NO SIMPLE HIGHWAY

The Life Journey of
a Childhood Trauma Survivor

A MEMOIR

Rory D. Kaplan

Publishing and Design Services: MelindaMartin.me
Editor: Gail Fallen, gail@mesanetworks.net

ISBN: 979-8-9891792-0-6

This book is a memoir. It reflects the author's memories of his experiences over time. Several names have been changed in the interests of privacy, some events have been compressed or omitted, and some dialogue has been recreated.

In memory of
my grandmother Sadie

ROADMAP

CHAPTER 1

Welcome to the World . . . and Brooklyn

Old black-and-white family movies were lying around in a closet for several years. When we finally located a projector and watched them, we were transported back in time. There they all were at my grandmother's house. My maternal great-grandmother, grandparents, parents, aunts, and uncles all appeared to be having a lot of fun while posing and joking around in front of the camera.

Suddenly, I saw myself enter the celluloid frame as a three-year-old boy. I had turned my small tricycle upside down, using one of the wheels to pretend to be driving a car. I held a clothespin in my hand, pretending to puff on a cigar as I was turning the steering wheel. In the next scene, I was wheeling a small baby carriage with a doll in it. I took the doll out, hugged it, put it back in the carriage, and started hitting it. Two questions came to mind: *Why was I doing that? And was I emulating my own experience?* Could it have started when I was so very young and in a baby carriage? I knew I had been physically and verbally abused as a child, but seeing that made me feel sick and ashamed, especially with other people watching the film. I wondered what kind of people would abuse a child of three or even younger. Unfortunately, those people were my parents.

I was angry upon seeing that, and it made me more determined than ever to dig further into the cause of the pain, fear, anxiety, and depression that had been plaguing me throughout my entire life. It led to a journey that took me back to Brooklyn, New York, where I was born in 1955.

Many interesting things occurred in the year 1955: Dr. Martin Luther King Jr. led a bus boycott in Montgomery, Alabama, a major event of the civil rights movement. The Interstate Commerce Commission ordered the desegregation of trains and buses. UHF television was widely available, costing around $100 for a set. The Brooklyn Dodgers had beaten the Yankees in the World Series, and the number one song on the pop charts was "Rock Around the Clock" by Bill Haley and his Comets.

Those early days in the Midwood section of Brooklyn were wonderful, especially in summertime. My grandparents' house was located on East 28th Street, just off Kings Highway. There was a subway stop on the corner, and it was only a short walk to the main shopping area, which offered a plethora of shopping opportunities. Several movie theaters, restaurants such as Dubrow's and Jahn's, and a variety of stores all lined "The Highway" from Ocean Avenue to Ocean Parkway.

One of my earliest recollections that something was wrong occurred when we were moving out of our apartment.

"Mom, what are you doing?" I asked as I watched my mother angrily ripping the wallpaper off the wall in the kitchen. I was four years old at the time, and I was frightened and confused at what I was seeing. My mother responded, saying, "We did not pay for this so that they can have it."

At that time, we were living in a three-room apartment on Kings Highway in Brooklyn and getting ready to move outward and upward to Sheepshead Bay into our own attached house. My mom, Marla, was a twenty-four-year-old stunningly beautiful woman. She and my dad were married in 1953 shortly before I was born. My dad, Louis, was a year younger than my mom, and he was an incredibly handsome man with movie-star looks. They were an amazingly good-looking couple.

Mom was the oldest child of four with two younger brothers and a sister. She and my dad married young, which was not unusual at the time, and they could not afford a place of their own. As a result, for the first three years of their marriage, they lived with her parents in their house. Those years were key as I grew remarkably close to my maternal grandparents, Myron and Sarah. My grandmother "Sadie" would remain a major influence throughout my life's journey, and my grandparents were for all intents and purposes my parents in the early stages of my life.

Grandma's house was shotgun style with a living room in front, a dining room in the middle, and the kitchen in the back, which opened to a porch and a small yard. The garage in the yard area would serve as my play area where I imagined building a go-kart and a super car. I would climb up the back of the garage to see the apartment buildings behind the house and the open area where residents would sit and relax. My curiosity led me to sometimes venture over to that side just to see what was going on. Even at an early age, I had a desire to seek out new people and places.

Grandma Sadie made the most of her small yard, and when not putting clothes on the line to dry, she would tend to her flowers, particularly the beautiful roses. She would do her household chores while Myron worked away at his dry-cleaning store on Flatbush Avenue near Brooklyn College. He was a diligent worker, working from 6 a.m. until 9 p.m. every weekday and Saturday until 6 p.m. He was only off on Sundays, and, even then, he would take a ride to the store to set up for Monday and often take me with him. I loved that store and was especially intrigued by the back area where the machines were. That is where the "presser" used a big ironing board that spouted steam out of a huge iron type of device used to iron the dry-cleaned items.

The inside of my grandparents' house was a wonderland to me at that early age. The dining room had a staircase to the right that led upstairs to three bedrooms and one bathroom. There were stairs to the right of the kitchen that would lead past a side entrance and down to the basement. A cubby area under the stairs was filled with boxes of books and other items—things that captivated my attention for hours on end. There were scrapbooks, a stamp collection, and my uncle's college textbooks. (He would later become a dentist.) His tennis rackets and golf clubs sat just outside across from the cubby entrance. There was a storage room in the front area which was packed with clothing items and smelled of mothballs and cedar. The back area contained a bathroom and washing machine, though most noteworthy (and scary) was an oil burner room. It had that big black tank and would scare the hell out of me when the burner would kick on.

The wonderland would turn into a terrifying place when I fell asleep. I was plagued with nightmares for many years, and one of the early ones was when I would be near that oil burner room. When it rumbled to life, I would then run down the hall and up the stairs to escape. Just when I would reach the top step, a woman's hand would grab me by the back of my neck, digging her nails into it. I would try to shout for help, but no words would come out, and I would wake up screaming. The women's hand looked just like my mother's.

Nightmares and night terrors are listed as some of the effects of childhood trauma. It took many years until I would begin to understand how deeply my siblings and I were affected by the parental beatings and verbal sadism we endured as children.

Much later in life I would learn that those early days, influenced primarily by my grandmother, created a foundation that would become a lifesaver. My grandmother was a wonderful, loving person and was my primary caretaker while living in her house until I was three years old. She had assistance from my great-grandmother (her mother), and according to my mother, the combination of those two helped her greatly, as she was young and admitted that she did not know how to be a mom.

The other prominent people in my early years included my grandfather, who, according to my parents, was an animal. My father said when he first met him, he thought he was a funny guy and he liked him. My mother despised him, and, many years later, I would learn why. Despite what I was told, he was good to me and the other kids. He would often take me to Coney Island for pony rides off the Belt Parkway and the carnival rides in Sheepshead Bay.

My maternal aunt and uncles were around most of the time, and they were all great to me, as I was their first nephew. My older uncle Herb was around for a while and then served our country, but I did not see him much during his time of service. Next was my uncle Hal, who was interesting and somewhat mysterious. He would spend some time with me, and, later in life, I saw pictures of him with me, and he always had a big smile on his face. I was maybe two years old, and he was around fourteen in those photos. I did not have an older brother, so I think, perhaps subconsciously, I thought of him in that way. In subsequent years he appeared to be a loner to the family and would spend most of his time in his room studying after enrolling in dental school.

My aunt Barbara was the youngest child and the closest to my age, and she also spent a good deal of time with me.

I remember when she was maybe seventeen, she acquired a new red Ford Mustang. She took me bowling one day, and, at the bowling alley, three guys tried to pick her up. She also took me to see the movie *West Side Story*, which I had wanted to see very badly. I listened to that album constantly and was fascinated by the gangs and the love story.

I loved them all, and, later in life, they played a role in my personal development. The best times were when the family would get together for holidays and when my dad, my uncles, and I would watch the Giants football games together on Sundays. Those were great times and provided me with a solid foundation. However, trouble was right around the corner.

CHAPTER 2

What's Going On Here?
Trouble in Paradise

That first really frightening nightmare and the others that followed were a sign that something was very wrong. While all was great during those early years, things started to change dramatically.

We moved into an apartment on Kings Highway when I was three years old, and though we were still close in proximity to Grandma's house, my parents were now on their own. I have only vague memories of living there. Those old home movies showed me riding a brand-new bicycle on the sidewalk in front of the building. The building itself was a short walk from the main area of Kings Highway, which was lined by several restaurants and retail stores. The candy store under the El train was similar to the one in *West Side Story* where the Jets gang would hang out. An old man stood behind the counter that was situated on the left side as one entered, across from a big display of candy that was next to a magazine and newspaper rack. Grandpa would buy me pretzels that a worker would take out of a circular container. Those would be washed down with a malted mixture of seltzer, milk, and chocolate syrup, blended in a green-colored "malted machine."

Grandpa would treat us kids exceptionally well, though my mother had major problems with him. I later discovered some very disturbing things about him that created conflicts between him and my mom, her siblings, and my grandmother.

My mother felt she was unwanted by her father due to her mother getting pregnant and the subsequent "forced" marriage. According to my mother and another source, my grandfather once punched my grandmother in the mouth, knocking out her teeth. He continuously taunted my uncle, who stopped talking to him, and took a full swing at my aunt when she was a teenager. He fortunately missed. I saw him punch an elderly man who was a tailor working at his store.

I do not know if all of those stories are true, though as a child I witnessed a few of them, which is bad enough. And surely they would have negatively affected my mother and would explain volumes about her emotional problems. I learned that the cycle of abuse stays alive and repeats in each generation until, and if, someone stops it.

Around a year after the Kings Highway move, my parents decided to move again, this time to an attached house in Sheepshead Bay. This is where my memories of the more serious abuse started. The men would play touch football on our block on Sunday afternoons. On Saturdays, they would be out doing chores, washing their cars and doing yardwork. My dad had to work on Saturdays. It made me sad to sit on the stoop alone watching the other kids help their dads.

My mother was very nosy, and if she heard the neighbors fighting, she would sometimes put a glass to the wall to try and hear what was going on. I remember one incident that occurred when my mother was playing Mahjong with her friends in the dining area of the kitchen. I thought it would be funny to imitate my mother, so I put a glass to my ear and the wall during the game . . . and the women all saw me. It embarrassed her that I did this in front of her friends, and I paid the price by receiving a beating, the first of many that would follow for me and my younger sister. While hitting us in fierce rage, she would also verbally attack us, saying the most vicious things. I was told later that this was a form of verbal sadism.

At four years old, I didn't know how to digest or react to getting pummeled and being told what a bad kid I was. I had no choice but to endure it, though the nightmares became a regular occurrence. I would see silver heads in my room and a witch across the street in the back of our house, where there was an inlet from Sheepshead Bay. I would see tidal waves coming from the bay up Knapp Street, which was around the block. I was a scared little boy not knowing when the next attack would occur.

When I turned five years old, I wanted to attend a nursery school that offered through the local elementary school the summer before kindergarten would start. Initially my mother was against it, but I persisted, and she agreed to let me go.

I remember one particular incident when I was in that classroom. I don't recall exactly what I did, but it was something disruptive. The result of whatever I did was being told by the teacher to go outside and stand in the hall. I waited for a little while and then decided to leave and walk the few blocks to get home. I opened the doors and went outside, only to suddenly realize that the area was surrounded by an iron fence. When I turned around to get back inside, the door was locked, so I had to wait there a long time until the doors opened at the end of the school day. I was trapped and just stood there, not knowing if or how long it would take until the doors opened. Once again, I found myself in a frightening situation. That was my first and last day at that school.

My dad was young at that time and struggling while trying to find the right career path. One day he came home early, and I was happy to see him. He told my mother he had lost his job and she verbally tore him apart.

"You're nothing but a truck driver and that's all you're ever going to be," I remember her saying. He did not respond, and that was the beginning of a pattern that would go on for years. My mother would berate him endlessly, and he would just accept it. It was troubling to witness her abusive behavior toward my father. He was the guy I looked up to—my hero—so I felt terribly sad for him.

My dad was more likeable than my mom and generally got along with most people. He loved to joke around and was well liked by all the local store owners. His sister, my aunt Sophie, told me that when he was a teenager, everyone in their Coney Island neighborhood loved him.

He was also my protector.

One day I was outside on my bicycle and another kid on the block was in front of me on his brand new one. I tapped into the back of it, and his father came running over and smacked me in the ass, saying, "I saw what you did, and you did it on purpose."

In those days it was somewhat acceptable for other parents to discipline someone else's kid if they saw them doing something wrong, but hitting was not okay. I went home and did not say anything, but my parents could tell there was something wrong. I finally told them that this guy Al hit me. The next thing I remember was seeing Al on the ground with blood around his mouth and three or four guys holding my father back. I was glad he protected me. It gave me a good feeling, like he loved me.

My mother's illness and behavior would wear away at him over the years, and he became increasingly like her over time. It was bewildering to his family, who my parents had cut off from all contact with our side of the family for many years. We were very close when I was a child. We would get together on a fairly regular basis until I was around fourteen years old. That's when it all changed. His only sibling was my aunt Sophie, and she, my uncle Simon, and my cousins reconnected with me years later. They told us they had no idea why they were cut off and that it troubled them for years. Their attempts to reconcile were rejected. My mother led the charge by creating some fantasy about how my aunt and grandparents had screwed my father financially by not setting him up in a business when my grandfather retired and sold a very successful trucking company. Their belief was that my aunt was given everything and my father was given nothing, which was untrue but became a self-fulfilling prophecy. My mother would vilify them constantly and yammer at my father about how bad they were; she even tried to get him to believe he was adopted. Although my cousin reached out to him when my grandfather died, he decided not to attend his funeral. My grandmother was so disgusted, she specifically cut him out of the will.

After my aunt reached out to me, we reconciled with that side of the family years later after my father died. They are all truly wonderful people and the total opposite of what all the venom my mother spewed forth would have had me believe.

At my aunt's unveiling ceremony a year after she passed, one person after another spoke about what a loving and positive woman she was. She and my uncle would often say how sad it was that we missed so many years that we could have had together as a family. I would tell them how we were at least fortunate to have had those few great years as a family. It breaks my heart how my mother destroyed that relationship as she did with every other one in her life and how my father, who was surrounded by good people, was eaten up by her mental illness.

When I spoke briefly at the ceremony for my aunt, I broke down talking about how much our reconciliation meant for me as it did for her. She never gave up in trying to achieve that, and I will always remember our times together and the regular phone calls we had until her passing. I would sometimes tell my wife, Ann, that I wished Aunt Sophie had been my mother instead of my actual mother. She thought I was joking; however, I wasn't.

Indicative of the situation was an incident that occurred one afternoon while my family was shopping at Fortunoff's, a high-end department store in Brooklyn. According to my mother, I was three years old at the time when somehow I became separated from her and my father. While I was lost, a young couple noticed me and realized what had happened. They were genuinely nice and bought me cotton candy as they brought me to the store employees. I remember thinking that they were going to be my new parents, and the strange thing was that I was good with it. When they found my real parents, I was disappointed to realize I would be going back to them.

Another disturbing incident occurred when I lost my eyeglasses. I was only six years old at the time, and, due to astigmatism, I needed to wear glasses to help correct a muscle weakness in my eyes. My name was pasted in gold letters on the glasses case to help identify me as the owner if I lost them.

One day, after coming home from school, I realized my glasses were missing. My mother went crazy and berated me screaming how "glasses cost money . . ." She forced me to keep searching everywhere in the house, so I looked behind dressers and under beds, desperately trying to find them. She wouldn't let it go, and one morning, before school, she told me to go outside and look for them. I was really scared because we had recently seen rats running around in front of our house. When she saw them, she was terrified and hid in the bedroom. She called Grandpa, and he came over before going to work to help calm her down. Knowing her own fear of rats, she sent me out to where they had been seen to try and find the glasses. I was scared but had no choice, so I pushed myself to go out there and walk around like an idiot, knowing there was little to no chance that they were there.

When I told Ann that story, she found it incredibly sad and said, "I can't imagine doing that to a six-year-old child and what that did to you." I remember feeling like I did something really bad, like I let her down and failed at being responsible. A few days later, someone found the glasses in school and notified us, as they apparently had fallen out of my book bag.

A pattern was developing in which the abuse was affecting how I felt about myself. The continuous verbal abuse made me feel like I was a bad kid and a disappointment. I felt the same way when I would hear her berate my father in a similar manner. Those feelings dig deep and can destroy people, and many never recover from them.

Despite what was happening at home, I was doing quite well at school. In second grade, I was placed in an Intellectually Gifted Child (IGC) class in which we were taught advanced subject matter, for example, the basics of geometry. The beginning of a of a two-pronged path was starting to emerge, one that I would walk down for most of my life. One side was the smart, sensitive, nice guy; on the other was a tough guy with an edge. I didn't realize what was really going on at that age and just kept going as a matter of survival. I lived through it the best I could while not knowing or understanding the devastation that was being done to my soul.

A key event that helped shatter the good aspects of the early good days occurred one Sunday afternoon at my grandmother's house. I was playing in the living room while my dad and grandfather were sitting around watching TV. We could all hear the conversation as my mother was talking to my grandma. She was verbally teeing off about my grandfather visiting his mother every Sunday.

"What kind of man does that?" she asked. Then she started berating my great-grandmother Devora, saying all kinds of vicious things about her. Devora was a Holocaust survivor whose entire family was murdered by the Nazis. It was only recently when my cousin told me the story; she then questioned how anyone could be "normal" after that. She told me that Devora had burned all her family pictures saying how all those pictured were put in the ovens.

I've speculated what effect that horrific trauma would have had upon the way Devora raised my grandfather . . .

how it had likely contributed in a major way to his abusive behavior which, in turn, would explain my mother's issues. Later, I was told by my aunt how much Devora and my great-grandfather Isaiah loved my mother, their first grandchild. I found pictures of them with my mother that seemed to reflect that love.

Despite their love for my mother, she had them on her list of people who were rotten. She would constantly try to turn my grandmother against my grandfather, pouring gas on the already existing fire of her disillusionment with him. At a certain point during my mother's rants, Myron erupted, screaming at her not to talk that way about his mother. My father, in response, came to my mother's defense and started arguing with my grandfather; he even threatened him. Myron told him to get out of his house, and when my father refused, he threatened to call the cops, which he ultimately did. The police arrived and diffused the situation. My father, however, brought it up for years afterward, questioning how Myron could call the police on him. He never questioned his own actions and threats against a much older man in whose home he was a guest. As a little kid, I was really confused by what happened. Initially, I thought it was a joke. Then I realized it wasn't. It was very painful seeing people you thought all cared about each other going at it to the point where the police got involved. A nice Sunday gone wrong without notice.

Another incident that captured the good times turning bad was when we spent a day at the circus. Barnum &

Bailey had brought their show to Madison Square Garden in New York City, and we had a wonderful time seeing all the performances of trapeze artists and the clown shows. We also saw the "freak show," which I did not like. The bearded lady, the giant, and especially the fat man scared the hell out of me. I think I started crying when I had to sit on his lap. We left with the flashlights they distributed as souvenirs.

When we returned to my grandmother's house after the circus, my mother; her younger sister, Aunt Barbara; and Grandma were all sitting around the kitchen table. I heard arguing, and suddenly my mother threw a mayonnaise jar at my aunt, which shattered against the wall. What had been a nice day had once again been destroyed by the unexpected actions of my mother. It became more and more difficult for me to relax and trust good situations, never knowing when or how an eruption would take place. I became more and more anxious, though I didn't understand why.

Looking back, I think that my uncle Hal would stay in his room most of the time because of the dissension my mother created. I think he knew how screwed up the family was, which is why he limited his time and interactions with them as much as possible. Years later, we were told the reason for his constant isolation was that he was studying for dental school. Maybe he really *was* studying. Who knows? My mother told me stories of how Hal had asked Myron for money to help pay for his schooling and Myron refused him. Whether true or not, he ultimately graduated and became a very successful dentist with a practice on 57th Street off Lexington Avenue in a high-end area of Manhattan.

My first experiences of family dysfunction were not pleasant, but they were only a small indication of things to come. Those experiences began during my early formative years that started out so well, while I experienced the love of family. Unfortunately, things took a bad turn thereafter. The severe effects of both the abuse and the dramatic change from a loving environment to an abusive one would significantly affect me in the years that followed.

The next step in my journey began on that note, with a move to Queens.

CHAPTER 3

Here Comes Queens

*H*alfway through my second-grade year, my parents decided to move the family to Queens. My mother had a cousin who lived in a town there called Floral Park. We visited her and the cousins a few times to check out the area and to help my parents decide if it would be the right place for us. Floral Park was at the tail end of Eastern Queens bordering Nassau County.

The major street running through it was called Union Turnpike. Small, Cape-style, detached houses were located south of the "Turnpike" that stretched down past the other major street, which was called Hillside Avenue. The western border of the neighborhood was Commonwealth Boulevard, and the eastern border was Lakeville Road. To the north of the Turnpike was a sizable garden apartment complex called Glen Oaks. There were around three thousand apartments encompassing similar borders to Floral Park and a neighboring town called Bellerose.

The occupants were mostly White, middle-class, Italian, Irish, and Jewish second-generation immigrants, working people who were parents of the baby boomers.

My parents decided it would be a good place to live for all the amenities and some other key factors. The surrounding area, and Queens in general, was much less congested than Brooklyn. There was an elementary school just down the block from our house and a junior high school only a few blocks away.

It appeared that the neighborhood would be a great place for us, and for the most part it was in many ways. However, as time went on, I would experience some of the negative aspects and bad characters hidden under the covers.

I enjoyed the spaciousness of the new house, and just playing in the basement provided some distance from my parents. I was now also allowed to ride my Royce Union English Racer bicycle in the street. In Brooklyn I was not permitted to do that due to the traffic and congestion. When the warmer weather came, I started to explore, and I took my first bike ride. As I rounded the corner, I stopped to look at an old house surrounded by a wood fence. It looked like a house you would see on a Western TV show and gave me the feeling like I was living in the country.

The park on the corner was an extension of the elementary school and was a big attraction for me and all the other kids. In the park and on our block we would play all sorts of games, including stickball, softball, handball, basketball, and touch football. We loved being outside, and, when forced indoors due to severe winter weather, we were creative in finding ways to entertain ourselves. We loved snowstorms, and they rarely prevented us from going outside. We would play until our feet and hands froze.

Stickball games on various blocks were quite common in those days. It was here that I developed an interest in baseball, the first sport I loved. Years later, I ran into a friend who lived a few houses down from me. He told me that he was first allowed to play with the older guys in the neighborhood only after I had moved in. I asked why and he replied, "Because you were so good that they let you play, and then they had to let me play too."

I was surprised to hear that because as a seven-year-old playing hardball in Little League, I could not hit the ball. Playing in front of crowds of parents was intimidating, and once you lose confidence, everything goes downhill fast. I played one more year and decided to quit. My father played baseball for his high school team and I never felt that I measured up to that. If he had taken the time to teach me some basic fundamentals, that may have helped me. However, he was always working, and the few times he asked to come to a game, I told him no because I did not want him to see me failing.

While the park on the corner was filled with kids playing, there was also something else going on. Older guys and girls who were members of a gang called the "Whelans," and their younger counterparts, the "Little Whelans," were also hanging out in the park. I was intrigued by them and used to sit on a bench to watch the guys play softball games. They would wear either sleeveless muscle shirts or T-shirts with their cigarette packs rolled up in their sleeves. The most common hairstyle for guys were the "DAs," i.e., slicked back and pushed forward in the middle with square backs. Jeans were held up with garrison belts, and you could hear the clicking of pointy shoes with taps as they strutted around. A few years later, "Beatle boots" became the rage.

Those guys looked tough and that impressed me. The girls were pretty, and, a few years later, when I was around eleven years old, one of the older ones would make out with me. I do not know why she did that, as her friends would look on and laugh. I did not understand, but I sure liked it.

The gang was made up of mostly tough Irish and Italian kids who were notorious in the neighborhood. An article in a local newspaper described a gang fight between the Whelans and some other local gang in which chains and other objects were used. Years later, I read on some message boards that the Whelans would sometimes chase long-haired hippies around trying to cut their hair; rumors ran rampant that the gang was also anti-Semitic. The gang was one of several around Floral Park and Bellerose, each claiming their turf, hanging out, and getting into fights and other mischief.

I think my attraction to the gang was tied to my obsession with the movie and music of *West Side Story*, the gang fights, and the love story of the handsome couple that ended in tragedy. My parents were a handsome couple who were child abusers. What should have been so "right" was turning out all wrong, as my mother's actions were progressively worsening. She started fighting with our neighbors and telling me to say vicious things to the people next door.

My sister and I were beaten severely and on a regular basis. Things would be going well when suddenly she would go into an extreme rage and attack one or both of us. She would slap us, punch us, dig her nails into our faces, and pull our hair while saying the most unimaginably terrible things about us. While it is not atypical for married couples to argue, my mother would verbally abuse my father. She would throw things at him, and, a few times, she tossed all his clothing down into the cellar.

At such an early age, I did not understand any of this and the effects it was starting to have on my sister and me. In addition to the anxiety of never knowing when my mother would go into a tantrum, I started to develop a significant amount of anger. I started to fight back verbally by cursing at her and saying insulting things to her. My sister was not that type of fighter, which may have made things worse for her in the long run. My brother was just a baby at that time, and he would grow up to be very mellow. Everybody reacts differently to that type of trauma. I was the fighter.

While I was still doing well in school, in the so-called "smartest" class every year, I was starting to act out. I got into fights and other kinds of trouble.

One day, shortly after we moved to Queens, I was in the park handball courts flipping baseball cards with a kid a year older than me, and we ended up in a fistfight. Once it started, we were surrounded by members of the Little Whelans gang who helped incite things and were enjoying it all. It went on for a while, and neither of us would give in as we were locked in a wrestling match. It ended when my mother looked down the block and saw the crowd gathered around two fighting kids, one of them being me at the ripe old age of seven.

I wanted to be like the other kids who were attending Hebrew school, so I asked my parents to let me attend.

My family was not religious at all. We never attended temple and did not follow any of the Torah laws and rituals. We honored the major holidays by having dinners with the family and did not work on the High Holy Days. We would light the menorah on Hanukkah, and that was about it. I knew we were Jews and different from Catholics, but I had no deeper understanding of what that meant.

I started at the school a few weeks late and had to make up work on my own. The teachings covered Jewish history, customs, law, and holidays, as well as the Hebrew language. There were services on Saturdays for the Sabbath and other services for the holidays. I was interested in all of it, especially the Hebrew language, which I was picking up very well. I arrived at a point at which I could read the Hebrew in the stories within our textbooks and comprehend much of what I was reading.

After a while I started to lose interest, and, by the third year, I had had enough. Things at home were bad as my mother was now under more pressure taking care of my three-year-old brother. My father continued to struggle with finding the right career, and the more pressure on the family, the worse her behavior and abuse became. By year four, the principal declared to my parents that I was "the worst behaved child in the entire history of the Hebrew school." I considered that an honor, as there were plenty of wise asses preceding me. To my relief, we mutually agreed that there would be no bar mitzvah and that I would leave the school.

Throughout this period, my fascination with the "tough" guys in the neighborhood continued. I was a voracious reader, and I found a book in the library about famous criminals. I was drawn to the chapter about the Ma Barker Gang and Alvin Karpis. It inspired me to form my own gang. I started getting into fights, which was common for boys to do at that time. One day after school, I punched an annoying classmate in the mouth and he ran home screaming.

At ten years old, I started to hang around with some guys who lived in another garden apartment complex in the neighborhood that was called "Langdale." Even at an early age, I was able to cross lines, and the Langdale guys were mostly Italian and Irish Catholics. It was the beginning of a pattern that would continue for the rest of my life: maintaining strong relationships across ethnicity and race.

We were just some young punks, and we decided to form a gang called the "Stone Boys." To join the gang, you had to pass the initiation of burning one of your own fingers with a lit match. We hung around the apartments looking for mischief. The worst thing we did was to climb onto the garage roofs of the apartments and rip the shingles off, throwing them at targets. The last time we did it, some guy came out with a dog chain and chased us away, so we never did it again.

At that time, I became friends with a guy named Jack Girardi, who was one of the funniest people I ever met. We crossed paths many times over the years, remaining friends even as we both shifted in and out of different social groups. He was a wild guy, though behind his comedic behavior, there was a lot of pain. He wound up on drugs, unable to get his life together, until he sadly passed away in his forties, never having a wife or family of his own.

Moving into that neighborhood exposed me to kids of other religions and nationalities for the first time. It was a wonderful place to grow up during a unique time. Despite the trauma of severe abuse and some of the craziness that took place there, the neighborhood provided me with a place of refuge outside my home. Lifelong bonds of friendship were formed with some wonderful people. I feel a connection with many of those people that is different and much deeper than that of just "some old friends." I believe that, subconsciously, those relationships became my family.

CHAPTER 4

Times are A-Changing

On a sunny, crisp fall day, we received the terrible news of the assassination of President John F. Kennedy. It was a very frightening and uncertain time for the country that remained in sort of a lull or depression after the shock of the assassination.

Shortly thereafter, something else occurred that many believe helped lift us out of the doldrums. One Sunday night in February 1964, the Beatles were introduced on the *Ed Sullivan Show*. I had never heard of them until a day when my family was driving back home from Brooklyn on the Belt Parkway. The car radio was on, and I heard a few songs that immediately caught my ear. "Those songs they keep playing sound great!" I told my father. I asked who the band was and he responded, "Oh yeah, they're a bunch of freaks with long hair." After the world saw them on *The Ed Sullivan Show*, things would never be quite the same again.

The British Invasion of music that started when the Beatles had appeared on The Ed Sullivan Show had a major impact on our neighborhood and many others. Many kids wanted to learn to play guitar, bass, and drums so they could form bands.

After a brief desire to play drums, my interest shifted to guitar. My dad, who at that time was driving a cab at night to help make ends meet, found me an acoustic guitar in a New York City pawn shop. It was a cheap brand named Stella, but it was a start.

We found a teacher who came to the house for my lessons. He was a college student with long hair, a thick mustache, and glasses. He resembled one of the "Peter, Paul and Mary" guys. He started to teach me folk songs and some Beatles stuff. I remember learning the chords and fills to the Beatles song "Help!" Things were moving in a good direction. Unfortunately, when the summer ended, he went back to college, and that ended those lessons.

The next teacher we found was a much older guy who taught me the fundamentals of reading music and some music theory basics. He pushed me to sing, which I did, even though I did not want to. I only wanted to play the music of The Beatles, the Stones, and many other emerging bands of the time. What he taught me never sounded like any of those bands.

One Friday night, the local junior high school held a dance for kids of any age. That opened the door for me to attend even though I was not yet in junior high. I was very excited to go and hear the band. I dressed in some outfit I thought was cool and walked the few blocks over to attend. I heard the music and entered the gym to see the band playing. They were very good, and I was in awe as they played songs like "Satisfaction," "I'm A Believer," and other popular ones. I was impressed; they all had long hair and looked like hippies. Their guitars were brands I craved, and the whole thing was overwhelming. Hearing them play so well made me feel like I just did not "have it," so I decided to give up the guitar, which was something I loved.

This was another disturbing pattern that was starting to develop. I was allowing perceived or actual failure to cause me to quit doing things I loved. I later gave up playing basketball and all organized sports for the same reason. My view, based on what I have learned as an adult, is that supportive parenting helps guide children through the ups and downs of various pursuits. Setting expectations and encouraging kids to do things to the best of their abilities while having fun is key to helping them enjoy whatever activities they are into. A cousin of mine who is a very talented and experienced musician told me: "Wherever you are at in your playing, there are always x amount better and x amount not as good as you are."

I wish I had received that advice as a young kid. It probably would have provided me with many more years enjoying the things I loved doing.

At this time, the broader society began to change, and our neighborhood was no exception. Long hair for guys, bell-bottom pants, puffed-out sleeve shirts, Beatle boots, miniskirts, and go-go boots for the girls were becoming the rage. The Vietnam War was dividing the nation; riots in Black neighborhoods, demonstrations, and marches were all having a huge impact. Despite all the turmoil, most of it did not directly affect us kids. Back then, we did not have the constant barrage of news and social media we have today. We were certainly aware of the troubling things our country was going through, yet we still were able to go about being kids. The one area that did impact us directly was race relations.

CHAPTER 5

A Race Thing

*W*hen I was a young kid, the presser in my grandfather's dry-cleaning store and the super at our apartment building were the first Black people I ever encountered. At that time the sections where we lived in Brooklyn were primarily composed of immigrant Eastern European Jewish and Italian families.

After we moved to Queens when I was seven years old, we went back to Brooklyn quite often to visit our family there. One time, on the drive back home to Queens, my dad's car was acting up as it kept stalling. He decided to take the back streets instead of the parkway just in case the car broke down completely.

We were driving through the streets of an area called East New York, which was a Black neighborhood. I had never been to or seen a place like that before, and I wondered what it was and who those people were. One thing that really stuck out to me was that in several windows there were sheets hanging instead of window shades or blinds. I asked my mother where we were, and she said, "This is a Black neighborhood where people are poor and live in tenements."

I did not quite understand what that meant; however, it disturbed me, and I remained curious. My relationships with the Black kids were interesting, unique, and something I was drawn to from when they first arrived by bus at our local elementary school. Our interactions were mostly positive, though there were a few altercations. To be fair, this was not really much different from my interactions with other White kids.

I think my interest and fascination with the Black kids, their culture and where they lived, was driven by my desire for exploration which can be a form of escapism. For me it was a subconscious coping mechanism in dealing with the constant abuse I was subjected to.

In 1954, the US Supreme Court deemed racial segregation in public schools to be unconstitutional. There was, however, a significant backlash against integration, and, in the '60s, busing was an attempt to desegregate the public schools in New York City. After much debate over whether busing was the right way to comply with the Court and achieve the goal, a decision was made to bus Black kids into our neighborhood from where they lived in Jamaica and Saint Albans in southeast Queens.

There were one or two Black kids placed in each class, and, for the most part, everyone got along. My mother told me that if I wanted to bring any of the Black kids to my house for lunch, it was okay to do so. That was important and one of the good things she did because it gave me a comfort level to become friends with those kids the same way I would with any others. Unfortunately, that was a big deal at the time.

Toward the end of the school year, there was a party day in school, and we were told that we could bring in our musical instruments. I brought an acoustic guitar; my friend Jason brought a snare drum and cymbal; and two of the Black guys—Ernie and Andrew—brought in a saxophone and a trumpet.

We were able to play well together without any preparation or practice. Andrew and Ernie were well trained in music beyond where I was, and their ability to play so well from reading the music made the whole thing happen. The teacher in charge was also quite impressed and sent us to several other classrooms to perform. I said to Jason afterward that I only wished these guys lived near us as our attempts at forming a band were awful. It was a wonderful experience, though, unfortunately, due to the distances between where we lived, we never played together again.

Society was going through the growing pains of integration, and, as kids in the city of New York, we were going through such pains as well. Until we started interacting, all we knew was what we saw on TV: the riots, crime, and demonstrations. We were at the forefront of breaking through the divide amid the nationwide turbulence.

Our interactions as kids were affected by what was happening in the adult world. When Dr. King was assassinated, some rioting ensued in the local junior high and other schools, as many Black kids were very upset. Minor skirmishes took place across racial lines, and there was animosity on both sides between some of the kids. However, there were also some very positive interactions across racial lines, and I experienced both.

In junior high, one of my classmates was a Black guy named Kenny who lived in a predominantly middle-class Black neighborhood called St. Albans. He and many other Black kids would take the bus every day to get from where they lived to the school in our neighborhood. My best friend Phil and I were friendly with the Black guys and girls in school, and, sometimes, on Saturdays, we would take two buses to get to their neighborhood so we could hang out with them. While on the second bus we were the only White faces, yet our curiosity and sense of exploration dispelled our fear of going on those adventures.

Kenny and his friend Kevin's houses were nicer than mine and many of the other houses in Floral Park. Kenny's parents had good, unionized jobs, and Kevin's dad was a state trooper. It brought home to me how absurd and destructive the racial prejudice and divide was and how poorly (and inaccurately) Blacks were being portrayed in the media. You rarely, if ever, saw the good side of that community depicted.

That year I also had a brief relationship with a Black girl whose name was Cynthia. I found her attractive and we would talk every day after school. She called me on the phone almost every night, and we really got along well. After school, we talked for hours until it was time for her to take the bus home. I wanted to make the next move with her, but I was hesitant. Then one day when we were outside the school after class, she looked at me and said, "Come here." Then she kissed me. It was magical!

One day she asked if I wanted to go to her house. I agreed and told her I would bring a couple of friends as I was a little scared to go there by myself. I was hoping that once we were there, the two of us could go off by ourselves and take things a little further.

My plan did not work out well. I knew that Cynthia had had a boyfriend in the past named Paul, who was eighteen years old. I assumed that her relationship with him was over as we were progressing with ours. When we arrived at the house, it was unsettling to see how shabby it was, and my first thought was how different it looked from our friends' houses in St. Albans. Her dad opened the door, and we entered a screened-in front porch containing an old, ratty-looking sofa. We said hello, and to my dismay she said, "I'd like you to meet Paul," who stepped out from behind the door. He said nothing and just glared at us.

We all proceeded to the basement not knowing what to expect, as there was the possibility we (or at least I) would get our asses kicked. Then, out of nowhere, Paul comes over to me and asks, "You want to f*ck Cynthia?"

"What?" I responded. "I never said that."

He repeated his question and then said "You wanna get boys? I can get boys, too."

He went back to his seat, and that was it. There was dead silence in the room, and it was so awkward we couldn't wait to get out of there. We were thrilled when the time finally came to leave. Cynthia's dad drove us back to the train station, and, on the bus ride home, not one word was spoken between the three of us. I never spoke to Cynthia again, thinking she set me up to make Paul jealous. Or perhaps he got word we were coming over and decided to just show up.

I'll never know the real reason, but that was one weird experience. I will never forget her and just wish her well wherever she is.

Many years later, while in my religious phase and eager to learn, I wound up spending a weekend in Crown Heights, Brooklyn, with a Hasidic family. It was an integrated community in which Blacks and Jews lived together, mostly in harmony at that time. After my weekend there, I would occasionally go back to study with a rabbi, and one time, while I was walking down President Street, I saw a Black guy coming down the street in the opposite direction with a boom box to his ear, blasting music. I was curious how the religious Hasidim would react to him, and, as he approached, they turned their backs to him. I thought that maybe it was an isolated incident, though I soon after realized it was somewhat common. Some of the religious Jews there were turning away and totally ignoring their Black neighbors.

That really bothered me, and it began to raise some questions in my mind. Jews had a long history of helping Black people during the civil rights movement. Some had even sacrificed their lives in the process. There were a few incidents of disagreement, though, for the most part, the two minority groups got along. Seeing the "religious" acting the way they did made me think about Willis Reed, the time I spent at his basketball camp, and the role model that he was. My earlier friendships with Black classmates from St. Albans and the girl from South Ozone Park had me wondering how this behavior could be of God.

In one of my later jobs at a bank, they had us attend training sessions, and one of them was entitled "Affirmative Action." The morning prior to the session, I thought about how boring it was going to be hearing about a bunch of rules for an entire day. It turned out that the instructor was an incredibly dynamic Black man who explained how many cultures had experienced prejudice in this country. The Irish, Italians, and Jews were examples of groups that had also gone through systemic discrimination at various times. He helped us understand how equality was not treating everyone the same—it was to treat everyone differently. That made me think about one of my Black colleagues who would often come to work late. People prejudged him without knowing his son had sickle cell anemia and that he would often be in the hospital with him all night. As a manager, it would be the right thing to treat him differently due to his predicament.

The main thing that impressed me about the session, however, was when he had us break out into mixed groups. He asked us to explain to the others in the group what our first experiences were with the other race. One Black girl in our group seemed really tough, and I wondered what she would say. When it came her turn to speak, she said, "My mother didn't play that shit; we weren't allowed to talk bad about White people." Another guy who had come to America from one of the Caribbean islands explained how he had not experienced any prejudice or racism where he came from and that it blew his mind when he got here. I spoke about how my mother gave me the okay to interact when the busing started and how important that was to me.

The whole activity showed me how one can easily misjudge people and how interacting and talking can really help to break down walls. In my personal interactions across racial lines, the best experiences were when walls would break down, something I always derived great satisfaction from. At my most recent job, my employer asked the staff to respond to a survey about how we thought racism could be countered in the workplace and beyond. My main suggestion was to "start interacting."

Perhaps, in some way, this was preparing me for the many cross-racial and cross-cultural interactions I would encounter later in my life. My first granddaughter is biracial, and sometimes when our arms are next to each other, I look at hers (which is darker than mine) and think to myself how absurd it is that the difference in our skin color is what this BS is all about.

CHAPTER 6

Major Transition–Sixth Grade

*G*reat changes in our society were affecting all of us in 1966 when I started the sixth grade. While I and many others were adapting to those changes, the abuse from my parents remained consistent, having a devastating effect upon my sister and me. My sister was three years younger than me and was dealing with her own hellish experience.

My confidence and self-esteem had deteriorated and was at a very low point. The Little League failure, seeing the great band at the dance, and my grandfather criticizing my guitar playing were all very damaging to me. In addition to the persistent beatings and verbal attacks, my parents' incessant fighting with the neighbors rose to new levels of craziness.

While my two-pronged path continued as I struggled with identity, I found solace in the neighborhood. Spending time with friends and family of friends provided some needed relief from the pressures of living in the turbulence of my own home. In many ways, the neighborhood became a surrogate family that helped me survive and ultimately recover from what could have been a much worse ending. It is well established that outcomes for victims of childhood trauma include higher rates of addiction, incarcerations, and a variety of psychological and emotional problems lasting into adulthood.

Sixth grade was my final year at elementary school, PS 115. On the first day of school, I was sitting in the schoolyard with a few friends when the buses pulled up with all the Black kids. We were curious and a little on edge in anticipation of this thing everyone had been talking about and was all over the news. One friend broke into a twisted chorus from the Rolling Stones song "19th Nervous Breakdown," substituting derogatory lyrics describing the Black kids. It broke the tension of the moment, but it was an indicator that there would be some problems in the implementation of the integration plan.

I had kissed a few girls by that time. The first kiss was during a game of spin the bottle. She was an attractive girl and I really liked her. I started to think about her romantically while listening to Beatles' and other love songs. That was the beginning of another coping mechanism for me, romantic fantasy. Our friendship was short-lived, as soon thereafter, her family was evicted from their Glen Oaks apartment for not paying the rent. It was so sad to witness the Marshalls removing all their furniture in front of the crowd that had assembled in the courtyard to watch. I felt very bad for her and her family, and, after that day, I never saw her again.

Another girl (whom I was not attracted to) would call me on the phone almost every night, supposedly to ask about homework. In reality, she just wanted to talk. During one of our conversations, she asked me to go to her house on a Saturday. I didn't want to go alone, so I asked my good friend Jason to go with me.

One autumn Saturday morning, Jason came to meet me at my house. I remember walking with him toward Violet's house wearing my suede Beatle boots. The crisp, brown leaves on the ground brought the song "California Dreamin'" to mind.

When we arrived, I was introduced to Violet's older sister Iris, who was very attractive. Iris had a boyfriend named Steve, and, almost immediately, they began to push me to ask Violet to "go steady." Then they asked me if I wanted to make out with Violet and if I knew how to do that. They offered to show me how to do it by doing it themselves in front of me. I thought that was strange, but I liked what I saw. The whole day felt weird, and, in the end, I finally conceded by asking Violet to be my girlfriend, and she happily agreed.

On the walk home, reality sunk in, and I told Jason I really didn't want her to be my girlfriend and that I wished it were Iris instead. I broke up with her two days later and did not interact with her again until I was around seventeen years old. Of course, at that time she was a knockout but in a relationship with a dirtbag guy named Tony.

Due to my fascination with gangs, I became part of a gang called the "Little Colts," which I hung around with during the sixth grade in the back of some of the Glen Oaks apartments near my house.

One day, while a group of us were walking in the back of the apartment complex, we crossed paths with some of these Noble Lord gang older guys. They started to have words with Charlie, one of our guys. I had no idea what the dispute was about, and I was shocked when one guy proceeded to beat the shit out of Charlie, leaving him on the ground with a bloody mouth. I was pretty shaken up seeing that and felt really sorry for Charlie.

That was the first of several fights and violent encounters I would experience throughout my teen years . . . and one or two incidents beyond. They would often leave me with mixed emotions. There was a side of me that was like my father, who had a violent streak. I wanted to be like him and the tough guys in the park. My other side was a sensitive one, and I would sometimes feel guilty after getting into fights. It just seemed to be a part of growing up living in the places we did. In my mind, winning, especially when the fight seemed justified, felt great, and losing was very embarrassing. I wound up with a winning record by far in the various fights I had. The major lessons I learned, however, were that there is always someone tougher than you are out there and that anything can happen in a street fight. Some of the toughest guys in our neighborhood lost street fights to opponents no one would ever believe could win.

One of my notable fights happened years later in a neighborhood bar called Hogan's on Hillside Avenue, a few blocks south of the Turnpike. Hillside was where my buddies and I had been hanging out for a few years, and we informally became known as the "Hillside Guys." That bar and another one a few blocks east called Herman's let us in starting when we were fifteen years old.

I had been sitting in a booth with a girl named Joanie, who was a very good friend. We were just talking, and I was somewhat drunk but feeling nice and mellow. Out of nowhere, some ice cubes hit me in the back of my neck, but it didn't hurt. I was feeling so good I did not react.

"What was that?" I asked Joanie.

She told me someone threw ice at us. I turned around to where I thought it came from and there, sitting in another booth, were Violet and Dirtbag Tony, her boyfriend. Tony was a tough guy who came from a broken home. When I first hung around with him years prior, there was no way I would want to fight him. Now, it was a few years later, and there we were. Joanie asked me if I was going to do anything about the ice, so I walked over to the booth and asked if anyone threw the ice. No one responded.

I asked again, stronger and louder, "Who threw the ice?" No reply.

One more time I asked in an angry tone, "Who threw the f*ckin' ice?"

Tony stood up and shouted, "I did!"

I saw red and responded by punching him in the face several times. Next thing I knew, others were joining in the melee, which was next to the pool table. Bodies were being tossed around and cue sticks were flying. I was promptly escorted out of the bar and told I was banned (along with one of my good buddies who was nicknamed HT). He had joined in to help protect me after Tony's friends got involved.

The funniest part of the whole story came out a few days later. One of HT's brothers told me that their older brother who drove for a local cab company had picked up some guy from Hogan's the other night.

When he saw his face, he asked what happened, and Tony replied, "Rory, HT, and those guys . . ."

HT's older brother was considered to be the toughest guy around at that time, and no one wanted any sort of confrontational encounter with him. I presume he was amused and somewhat proud of us when he heard that we kicked some ass. He always seemed to like me, though I'm not sure why. I was good friends with his three brothers and his sisters and spent time at his house. His mother liked me, as I was always respectful to her. Regardless of the reason, I was just glad he never kicked my ass.

Identity issues often plague victims of child abuse. In my teen years, I felt like I was living between two worlds. Getting into fights, hanging out with a rough crowd, and getting into trouble was one world. The other world was rooted in my early years when I had experienced the love from my grandmother and the relatives living in her home. Interest in sports and friendships with nonviolent studious guys and girls left a positive impression on me. It is common for teens to struggle with identity. For me, the contrasting worlds were a continuous source of pain and confusion that lasted for years.

On the less turbulent side, I started to learn how to play basketball in my friend Mitch's backyard after his parents had a concrete court built there. His older brother Matty, whom I really admired, started teaching me and a few other friends how to play. Matty was a very smart guy. He was also a good athlete and involved in student government, eventually becoming the class president of our high school. He was obviously very different from the tougher guys, and a part of me wanted to be like him and his friends.

Basketball was a new sport for me, and I really got into it. In order to teach myself more about how to play, I started taking books out of the library that explained positions and types of shots. I began going to the park near my house and playing on those courts as much as possible. I would also occasionally go to the gym at PS 115 after school, where the junior high team would practice. There were many Black players on that team, and seeing the way they played was very exciting.

Despite some positive experiences like discovering basketball, things at home were continuing to deteriorate. My parents' relationships with the neighbors had reached horrible levels of conflict. My sister and I were still beaten on a regular basis. We never knew when my mother would fly into a rage over some meaningless or nonexistent "bad" thing we did. They would fight with each other; usually, it was my mother berating my father over some perceived offense. A few times she threw all his clothing into the basement and threw objects at him. There was constant conflict in our home, and what was extremely disturbing were their threats to send my sister and me to a mental institution.

Some experts in the field of child abuse refer to that type of abuse as "soul murder."[1] Looking back, I can understand why. However, as a kid, I only knew it was bad. But I also recognized that there was nothing I could do about it. Feelings of hopelessness and anger started to develop. It got to the point that we knew another rage and attack would happen; we just didn't know *when*. It was also confusing how there would be times when my mother could be very nice and charming. She loved books and movies and would comment when she was moved by a story. She would feel sorrow for certain characters and groups of people. She was up on politics and current trends of the day and would voice her opinions regarding them.

The two drastically different sides of her caused me to not trust her, but I also didn't trust my father. He would follow along with her on everything. There were times when I would confide in them and a day later get attacked physically, verbally, or both. It was analogous to playing a slot machine. You start winning a little bit and then think it's your night, and you're going to win big. You keep playing and, for a while, it's good. Then, suddenly, it goes the other way, and, in most cases, you lose it all. That's what it was like with them. Many times, I was fooled into trusting them, only to come out on the losing end. My ability to trust others was negatively affected and has always been a challenge.

ↄ

In the meantime, I was still getting into trouble in different ways. Nothing very serious, just a few fights now and then and general mischief. By today's standards, I would probably be considered a choir boy.

One time, word spread that we, the sixth graders in PS 115, were going to fight another school—PS 186—located in the neighborhood on the other side of Glen Oaks. We were ready to go at it that afternoon when the school principal got word of it. Cops were around after school to break it up, so it fortunately never took place. When the crowd dispersed, I wound up walking away with a guy from the other school named Joey Galioto. We struck up a conversation and subsequently became good friends.

A few other incidents occurred that continued the disturbing trend of my rebellion. At that age, I did not understand why I did certain things, and it would take years until I did. I deeply regret anything I ever did to hurt anyone in any way due to my actions back then. Later in life, I apologized directly to some people I was able to find on social media or elsewhere. Some did not remember the incidents in question. Others were very forgiving, or no words were required when we reconnected as adults and became friends via social media. Our childhood days were well in the past, though I was relieved to clear the air.

The end of sixth grade had finally arrived. It was the conclusion of a tumultuous period of suffering the abuse and good times all mixed together. Upon graduation, a big question was who would make it into the Special Progress (SP) programs in junior high school.

I looked at my report card and saw that I not only made the SP program but was given the choice of skipping the eighth grade by going into the "two-year program." The other option was to go into an advanced study "three-year program," and still others were only given the option of the three-year program. It was confusing how a few brilliant kids were only given the three-year option. I was gratified to make it into the program, and, after discussing it with my mother, we decided on the two-year program.

The "foundational" years were ending, and they had been a mix of good and bad times that brought me through various difficulties and mixed emotions. I had experienced puberty, turmoil at home, verbal and physical abuse, acting out, street fights, my first interactions with girls, developing interest in music and sports, and ending on a high note scholastically. The abuse I endured, however, left emotional scars that would continue to plague me for years to come.

CHAPTER 7

The Good and the Bad

J unior High School (JHS) 172 was located only a few blocks from my house and served grades seven through nine. Prior to attending the school, I was familiar with the outside area, which had a park on the south side located on 82nd Avenue. It was a typical New York City park, with a "park house" and a flagpole next to it which would fly the American flag. Surrounding that were seesaws, swings, monkey bars, park benches, a small but full basketball court, and the extremely popular handball courts.

I did not know what to expect on my first day of seventh grade at JHS 172. I walked the few blocks to school thinking I looked cool wearing my new paisley shirt and Beatle boots. When I reached the school block, I looked to my right, and there was Tony Galioto, my friend Joey's older brother. He was a guitar player in the band I saw a year earlier. He had long black hair down to his shoulders and was wearing a suede vest with his arms around two girls. Seeing that was a bit deflating, but I proceeded. Welcome to junior high!

I was placed in a 7SP class under the two-year program where I was among very smart kids. The program required maintaining a minimum 75 percent average across all subjects. While I was able to meet that standard all year, my main interests were music, basketball, and girls . . . in no particular order.

I do not remember exactly how I became good friends with a guy named Dan Harwood. He was a friend among several that I had at the time, mostly Jewish guys that had remained friends from the previous years in PS 115. Some of my other friends were a little wilder, and then there were the kids from the other three elementary schools in the area all converging in the new school. I was somewhat on the nerdy side being in the SP, but I also had that other side within me that, as far as I could determine, most, if not all, the other "nerds" did not possess.

The anger, low self-esteem, and depression all stemming from the abuse was the other side. That age is challenging enough to go through under "normal" circumstances; however, for me, it was extremely difficult. The things kids go through and experience at that age were magnified for me, yet I only had a vague sense that something was not right. I did not understand the deeper impacts of what was going on and the effects they were having on me. Somehow, I kept going and found solace in my friends, interests, and the neighborhood.

Toward the end of my seventh grade year, my parents decided they would rejoin a local country club, one that we had belonged to the previous year that I hadn't liked. It was really just a pool club, offering a large outdoor pool and surrounding area with a snack bar and jukebox. The building was a catering hall you would walk through from the parking lot to get to the locker rooms and then out to the pool. Downstairs, in the basement, was a handball court, some exercise equipment, boxing gear, and a basketball court. It was owned by a Jewish businessman who owned other buildings around the neighborhood and had a reputation of being a tough guy.

My parents were doing a little better at that time, and my dad, who was in the prime of his looks, was getting some acting jobs. He would still drive a cab at night while doing some acting when he could get work. He was an extra on the movie *Hello Dolly*, a stand-in and double for Rock Hudson and Clint Eastwood in various movies, and had a few bit parts on the TV series *Peter Gunn*. On weekdays, my mother would drive my siblings and me to the club, and, for the most part, she seemed to enjoy it there. She did complain once when she thought my father and a very cute woman who wore low-cut bikinis were getting a little too friendly. My father would attract women wherever he went, though as far as I could tell, he always remained faithful to my mother. But who knows?

My dad would play paddleball with the other men there on the weekends. A few times they had mixed drinks by the pool, which led to some wild and funny antics. Both my parents were having a good time, and, for a change during that summer, we almost seemed like a normal family.

During the prior first year of our membership, I was forced to go to a few nighttime activities that I hated. I was at that awkward puberty age, chubby and self-conscious. I would wear a T-shirt at the pool because I thought I was fat.

One day by the pool, I noticed two very attractive girls tanning on the chairs in front of me. They were wearing lip gloss, and I thought they were so pretty and, for some reason, that they were younger than me. I concluded that they were way out of my league and would never be interested in me. In my mind, the song "Younger Girl" by the Critters would always be associated with those girls.

The following year, I had matured a bit from that awkward stage; I was looking better and feeling good about myself.

One day I was downstairs shooting baskets when a girl walked up to me while I was playing. We struck up a conversation, and she even tried to make a few baskets. It turned out that she was one of the pretty girls I had noticed the summer before. Her name was Amy, and I thought she was beautiful. She had very long, dark hair and was short and petite with strong and pretty facial features. I was very attracted to her but still thought she was out of my league.

As the summer progressed, we were spending more time together as friends. We would play Ping Pong® on the tables situated outdoors in an area near the pool. I was pretty good at it, but I would let her win points and played softly against her.

I became friendly with one of the guys there named Aaron, and one night I went up to his apartment in Deepdale Gardens to hang out. We got to talking about the girls at the club, and Amy's name came up. I told him I liked her. He asked me if he should call her without telling her I was with him to see if she liked me. I reluctantly agreed, but I was prepared for the worst. He told me she said she did like me, and I made him swear he was telling the truth. On my walk home, I was sky-high. As a music lover, all these great love songs would have me thinking about her: "Never My Love," "Here, There, and Everywhere," "Younger Girl," and "You Didn't Have to Be So Nice." It was the romantic fantasy of a thirteen-year-old.

Amy, Marcy, and several other kids at the pool were from a neighborhood just north of Glen Oaks called Little Neck and Deepdale. Though it was only a short distance from our neighborhood, it was like going to another country. Interacting with the kids there were the first explorations for those of us starting to venture out of our immediate neighborhood. Little Neck Country Club was situated between the two areas; that helped to bring about those interactions.

One day in the basement where we would hang out and smoke cigarettes, I was with four or five of the girls, and we decided we would play a kissing game. The result of that silly game was I got to make out with each girl in a closet. For some reason, when it was Amy's turn, and we kissed for the first time, it was different. First kisses were always good, but there was something really magical about this one. I had never experienced anything like that before, and it sent me over the moon. I became even more infatuated with her.

Amy and I made out a few more times before that summer ended. One day at the pool, I agreed to meet her and two other girls that same evening. As there would be more than just Amy, I asked my friend Joey to go with me to meet them. It was a quiet summer night, and we were very excited to spend time with those girls. Joey was so impressed at how pretty the three of them were that he mouthed the word "wow'" as we walked behind them toward the Glen Oaks Apartments.

We decided we would go to my house, though when we arrived there, I declined to bring them inside. I was always hesitant to bring friends home, not knowing what to expect from my parents, even though the rare times I did bring someone into the house, they were very charming.

My mother would often ask why I never brought friends over and I would not tell her why. The other reason was that our house had old carpeting worn in many places and the sofas were torn and I was ashamed of that. So instead of going inside, we decided we would make out while outside. Amy and I kissed under the light of a streetlamp while Joey did the same with one of the other girls. The summer night was so quiet and peaceful as we walked them up 260th Street past the Oval back home. It remains as one of the most memorable and magical nights of my early years.

Summer ended, and I would continue to visit Amy for a few months. For some reason, I always took a friend with me, either Dan or Joey. She was home alone while her parents were at work and we would just hang out in her apartment. I was so young and basically blew the opportunity to continue with at least a friendship.

I ran into her one more time in a local deli after I had just finished playing basketball with a friend. I noticed she and her parents sitting at a table in the back area. She made a motion as if to say hello, and I ignored her. When we finished our meal, I just left. Part of the reason was that I had braces put back on my front teeth after not having them on when I was with her in the summer. I was embarrassed and did not want her to see me like that.

Even though I was the main cause of destroying our brief relationship and friendship, I maintained the romantic fantasy. It was almost like I wanted to have a broken heart and subconsciously wanted to be rejected. That type of emotional pain was a comfort zone, which may explain why I was turned off to some very attractive girls who were attracted to me.

Many years later, I found her sister somehow online. We exchanged some messages and she mentioned it to Amy, who remembered me. According to her sister, she said, "He was sort of my boyfriend, but we were very young."

She's living her life, and I am living mine, and I hope life has treated her well. It was never meant to be, and I realized when I was older that I created the romantic fantasy as a coping mechanism to counter the pain and suffering caused by the abuse. The fantasy took me away from the beatings, fighting with neighbors and family members, and the sadistic verbal attacks that my sister and I had endured for years while growing up in our house.

თ

Basketball became everything to me as I moved through seventh grade. I played whenever and wherever I could: after school and night centers at the school gym, outside in all kinds of weather . . . it didn't matter. I would often go to the outdoor courts at PS 115 down the block from my house and play alone until someone else showed up for some one-on-one games. Like so many others, I would pretend to be on the Knicks or the St. John's college team. I would pretend to be other players (i.e., Bradley from the corner, Reed inside turns and hits, and so forth).

It was an escape from the drama and pain at home. While playing on those courts, I could see my house a short distance away, and occasionally glancing at it would give me a strange feeling. I wished things could be normal, though they weren't. My father played basketball with me maybe once or twice, as he was always working or too tired. But he did do something for me that changed my life in a good way, at least for a brief time: He obtained tickets to a New York Knicks game.

I became a Knicks fan early in the 1968–69 season. Back then, the only televised road games were on

Wednesday nights or Saturdays. On weekends, ABC would feature a game of the week, showing teams like the Celtics, 76ers, Lakers, and others. Knicks home games were only available on the radio. I started to listen to the games sitting in my kitchen where we had the family radio during the school winter recess. That was my introduction to Marv Albert, the famous, exceptionally talented announcer who made listening somewhat enjoyable as the only alternative when games were not televised.

My dad and I got in the car for the ride into Manhattan, which he knew how to do well from driving his taxicab there at night. He let me listen to my radio station so I could hear the songs I liked. He mimicked in a negative way the spoken lyrics in the song "I'm Gonna Make You Love Me" by The Temptations and the Supremes. Perhaps that is why I clearly remember hearing that one in particular from among the other Motown songs we heard that night.

We made it to what is referred to as the world's greatest arena: Madison Square Garden. I had only been there once before for the circus when I was around five years old but never for a sporting event. I was expecting it to be somewhat like what I experienced at a few Yankees and Mets games. I was shocked when we entered and saw how small and intimate the setting was in comparison to the baseball stadiums. The colored-coded seats separated the tiers from courtside up to the blues in the "nosebleed" section. We had good seats behind one of the baskets, maybe ten or so rows back.

It was magical when the Bullets came out in their black-and-orange uniforms. Jack Marin, Gus Johnson, and Earl the Pearl were among them. A minute or so later, to the roar of the crowd, out came the Knicks in their white, blue, and orange uniforms. Willis Reed, Clyde, and Cazzie Russell led the way.

The energy of the crowd was something one can only experience in person. Every foul call against the Knicks was like a burst of negative energy sweeping through the arena, while a foul call against the Bullets was met with a gust of positive energy. I was fixated on Earl Monroe, seeing him work his magic against Clyde. He would post him up in the corners, turn and fade away, and hit nothing but net. When the Knicks would go on a run, especially some fast breaks after steals by Clyde, the place went wild. The Knicks won the game against a formidable team that was a mirror image of themselves. It was unforgettable for me and also good to experience it with my dad as it was one of the few good times we had together.

When we left my dad wanted to get something to eat so we went to a Nedick's on 34th Street, right across the street from the Garden. It was a fast-food burger joint like Nathan's and was packed with people trying to place orders to get their burgers and fries. My dad was an imposing figure standing at 6'3". He told me to wait as he moved in toward the counter to get the food. I had the program we had purchased at the game that I was looking forward to reading once I got home. While waiting, I held it at my side and suddenly felt a tugging on it from behind. I turned around and glanced at a Black kid who seemed to be a few years older than me. He was actually trying to steal it! I held on to that thing for dear life, more afraid of what my father would do than of actually losing the cherished item.

The next day, while reading through the program, I saw an advertisement for a basketball camp run by future Hall of Famer Oscar Robertson. To be taught by pro players and coaches, *wow*! Though my game and skills were improving, I thought that going to a camp like that could really help advance my game. Upon further reading, I noticed that Willis Reed also had a camp. The cost of $125 for one week was not cheap at the time, and my mother was always opposed to sleepaway camps, which those were. It was a longshot, but I really wanted to do it, and, after some negotiating, my parents agreed to let me go. That would turn out to be an important decision that I hoped would work out well for something that meant so much to me.

After much back and forth, I decided to attend Willis Reed's camp instead of Oscar's. My dad and I went to Modell's on Jamaica Avenue in Queens to purchase all the items that were required to attend the camp. "Mo's," as it was called, had everything I needed, and, in particular, the must-have Converse All Star sneakers. The bus would be leaving from Madison Square Garden, where parents were to drop off the kids. I was a little nervous but excited as Willis would be meeting all the families and kids there to ensure things started off well. I would ultimately learn that is how he would run the entire camp; he really knew what he was doing.

After a few hours on the bus, we arrived at the New York Military Academy in Cornwall, New York, where the camp would be held. We were assigned individual rooms with two single beds in them. I had a roommate, and I don't think we spoke more than ten words to each other the entire week. The accommodations were adequate, though not elaborate by any means, and the biggest concern I had was that there were no stalls around the toilets in the centralized bathroom. I presumed that was the military way, though this was not very comforting. The whole week I saw only one person on the bowl. Obviously, there were a lot of constipated kids there . . .

Showers were communal with a bunch of guys all in there together. It was weird, but it was what it was.

The central meeting place was the big gym where instructions were provided, and various guest speakers would address the kids. Intramural teams were put together for competition that would lead to championships at the junior and senior levels. Pickup games would take place in the afternoons between the pros, college players who were counselors, and some of the really good senior players from among the kids. In the mornings, separate groups of kids would move from one basket to another learning different components of the game (i.e., how to dribble, rebound, shoot, make various moves, and play defense). The intramural games would take place during the afternoons.

My first night there, I reached out while I was sleeping to feel for my dresser that was next to my bed at home. When there was nothing there, I was a little upset, as I was only fourteen years old and had never slept away from home before. I was a little homesick, and the next day while at one of the baskets learning a drill, I thought about how I really wasn't enjoying things there and just wanted to go home.

Suddenly, a bright yellow Cadillac Eldorado pulled in near to where we were. Out stepped Walt Frazier, one of my idols, who was perhaps the greatest Knick to ever play and a future Hall of Famer. I was starstruck and immediately felt better. Later that day, he was nearby in the gym talking to a few kids and I really wanted to go over and talk to him, but I was too shy and couldn't do it. He addressed the entire group later in the big gym. He was a total class act—an amazing athlete and a person who had a positive impact on me at that very impressionable age.

Bob Lanier was still in college at the time and was working as a counselor at the camp. He was huge at 6'11" and was scary to watch during box out drills. He and another giant would fight each other under the boards for a rebound to show us kids how it should be done. In a shooting drill, I took my turn, taking a shot that I missed, and Lanier said, "Arc the ball, man."

My next time around, I did that and made the shot to which he said, "You got it, you got it!"

It was something I never forgot. Not only did he teach me how to shoot the right way, but to be taught by a future Hall of Fame NBA player was really something.

Toward the last day of camp, Willis told us that the camp would provide postcards for us to send to our parents. They would be invited to come up to the camp on the last day to pick us up instead of meeting the bus in New York City. I thought about it and decided not to send the card. I played well up there, but I was not a star, and I did not want to have my parents see that. I didn't want to disappoint them and have them see me fail or not really excel at something.

My parents were quite surprised when they and only a few other parents were at Madison Square Garden to pick up their kids. They either never understood or had no control over how their actions deeply hurt their children. They did not know how to be parents, nor did they know how to live and appreciate their own lives. Really sad for them, but sadder was the emotional damage they did to my siblings and me.

After my return from camp, I started using the new skills I had learned there. In a 1-on-1 game, for the first time, I beat a friend and former teammate from the church team who was very good. He shook my hand and told me how much my game had improved. I developed a very good outside shot and knew how to play defense and rebound. I also developed some moves to create my own shot, and I was feeling good and confident about my goal of making the junior high team.

One afternoon, a guy named Wade (who had been a teammate on my seventh grade team that won an intramural championship) was in the gym at the after-school center. He was a tall, exceptionally talented player who was generally viewed as the best player in our school. He was also personally a great guy who had devoted himself to playing ball and staying in shape in order to be as he once said, "a ball player."

We agreed to a 1-on-1 game and really went at it. I was hitting almost every outside shot I took, and he was posting me up. We battled it out, and the game ended with him beating me by only two points.

After the game, he said, "I want you to be my starting forward."

"Wade, I didn't even make the team yet!" I replied.

"No, man, you my starting forward," he said.

After the camp, I also excelled at the night center, winning a foul shooting contest, hitting thirteen out of fifteen, and competing at a high level against others in the 3-on-3 games played there. I was very much looking forward to playing on the school team with Wade.

The first day of tryouts I did okay; however, I did not distinguish myself and nothing I did stood out. That night, prior to the next day of tryouts, I was lying in my bed telling myself that I had to make this team. I had to go out and play the way I knew I could. Failing was not an option.

A guy named Ernie, whom I had played against previously in the intramural league, was our point guard during the tryout scrimmage. He was a head and shoulders guy who would look one way and pass the other. He saw

I was open in the corner and hit me with a no-look pass. I fired away and hit the shot. We did the same thing four more times. I played good defense, allowing only one guy I guarded to hit a shot. The coach called off the names of the fifteen guys who had made the team and my name was called. I was so happy and thrilled to have made it, thinking that this was finally something I was really good at. All the hours of practice in the schoolyards and gyms and at camp had paid off, and I felt pretty good about myself.

We had one practice, and the only thing I remember is not catching a pass from another player. I was not concerned, as I made the team and was hoping to start and have a good run. At the end of practice, however, the coach said he had to cut the team down to twelve and that he would post the names of the final team the following day.

After a restless night, I got to school and asked my classmate and friend Kenny, the guy from St. Albans, to go with me to check the bulletin board where the names were posted.

"Come on," he said, "you know you made the squad."

I responded that I wanted to be sure.

He accompanied me down the stairs, and I could feel my heart beating rapidly as we approached the board. I looked up and down the list and said, "Ken, I'm not on the list."

"What?" he asked, as he too scanned the list.

We were both shocked. My heart sank, and I felt like crying, though I held it back. Kenny was a good friend and sought to console me because he knew I got a raw deal.

I told my parents, who immediately blamed the coach. It was interesting that three White kids were cut, and one of the other two was a tall and lanky guy who eventually made the JV high school team. I had played with him in a Northeast Queens 3-man tournament, and we did well together. The other guy was an exceptionally good all-around athlete who eventually was All-City in baseball and had a tryout with a major league baseball team. Some of the Black kids who made it were not as good as we were, and one kid who made the team I would go on to destroy one-on-one in the park. The other guys who made the team were two of my close friends who knew I was better than they were and that I was probably in the top five in the school.

It all seemed very unfair, and parental guidance for a child who encountered such a situation for the first time would have helped. However, that would not be the case with my parents as they sought someone to blame and wanted to go up to the school to complain. I did not want that, and I made it very clear to them that I did not want to be put on the team because my mommy complained.

I was destroyed by what happened, especially after going to the camp. I lost all my confidence and even briefly joined the local Jewish center team. We had one practice game at another team's gym and I scored twenty points in the first half, playing the way I knew I could. But after one team practice, I just did not have it anymore. My dream of eventually playing for the Van Buren High School team was over. I left that practice knowing I would never go back.

As I walked back home through the backs of the Glen Oaks apartments. I thought about the camp, watching Dave Stallworth, Bob Lanier, Willis Reed, and Clyde play. I wondered what had happened to that world of joy and happiness I knew just a short time before . . .

What had given me a chance to make the team in the first place was what happened in the SP program. My mother and I decided that I would accept the two-year program that I was offered. It wound up being a poor decision for a variety of reasons. The thinking was, *Why not finish school a year early?* It was a decision that was not well thought through.

Seventh grade was okay, as the full acceleration of the program had not yet kicked in. I was required to maintain an overall minimum of a 75 grade average. The class had a good mix of kids, some nerds but some cool ones as well. I had a good social life, being good friends with Dan who lived in Glen Oaks. He was an interesting guy and we were alike in many ways, both of us having some deep-seated anger issues, and we both loved basketball.

On Saturdays, Dan and I would go to a local luncheonette on Union Turnpike called the Village Glen. There we would sit, smoking cigarettes, eating apple pie or corn muffins, and drinking cherry Cokes® while listening to songs like "White Room" by Cream, "Magic Carpet Ride" by Steppenwolf, and others. We would exchange albums by Jimi Hendrix and Janis Joplin as music remained a huge interest of mine, though I had stopped playing guitar. Dan was the one responsible for getting me onto the church basketball team, and he encouraged me to play in the baseball Pony League when I was fourteen. We didn't have a care in the world back then, except for our home lives.

The beatings and verbal abuse of my sister and me continued to occur on a regular basis. In one incident, I had told my mother I needed new jeans. She refused to give me money because I had bought two pairs of wild-looking pants as that style was popular for a while. They looked good in the store, but I felt like I looked like an idiot with them when I got home. One had brown and black squares and the other pair was yellow with blue stripes. I refused to wear them because I was self-conscious and would rather wear one pair of jeans forever than those pants in public.

One morning before school, we got into a big argument over this. My father was home and, being the enforcer, he got involved. He was threatening me, and I would always fight back. One word led to another, and I pulled out a knife I had bought from some guy in school. I was never really going to use it, but, at that point, he probably thought I might. He tackled me and twisted the knife away. He was a big, strong, tough man who would beat his children when needed, as in his mind he was defending his wife.

My relationship with him was always strained. He wasn't around much because he was always working. I learned my work ethic by observing him from an early age, which was at least one of a few positives. He was a personable guy who enjoyed schmoozing with neighborhood store owners, and he always had stories from his adventures driving a cab in the city at night. I think I developed those qualities of personability and storytelling mostly from him.

The downside was that he was never there when I needed a father. He was always stressed out, dealing with my mother's craziness, financial problems, and working two jobs. He would come home from work, and my mother would fill him in on the issues with the neighbors. On weekends, they would sit around, and my mother would work him up into a frenzy regarding his family and hers . . . how rotten everyone was and how they were out to get them. It was like some sort of persecution complex.

When they ran out of others to verbally trash in their hateful way, they would turn to my sister and me. My mother would start going down a list of all the things we were doing wrong and how bad we were. The end result would often be our parents busting open the doors to our rooms and threatening, yelling, and screaming at us. The last step would be hitting us with fists, scratching our faces, and pulling our hair while saying horrible things in the process. This went on for years, and the scars it left were deep.

There's a proverb that bad things come in threes, so at that point, while in junior high, I was up to two: I had and lost a relationship with a beautiful girl and made and was then cut from the basketball team despite the overwhelming consensus that I deserved to be on it. The third strike was what I would call "the SP fiasco."

As I said before, my priorities at that time were basketball, girls, and music, in no particular order. Hanging out in the neighborhood with a variety of friends encompassed all of them . . . and some mischief as well. I didn't want to be a nerd, so I hung around with some tough guys along with the more studious types. School and being considered "smart" was not a high priority or even on my true agenda.

In the two-year SP program, students would skip the eighth grade and go right from seventh to ninth. In my case, ninth grade started out okay, with mostly the same classmates as the year before. They were studious and considered to be on the nerdy side. I never really fit in socially with most of them. There remained a core group from elementary school whom I felt a strong bond with. They were smart kids, mostly Jewish, who also had a little bit of a wild streak. Dan was my best friend at that time, and he was wild like me. Joey Galioto and others who I mostly hung out with were not in the nerd world. Joey had been with me on that magical summer night when I took him up to Deepdale Gardens to meet Amy and the other girls.

Dan and I were often getting into minor mischievous adventures. One time he told me that his father, when referring to me, said: "When I get a hold of that black-haired bastard . . ." because of something we had done that ticked him off. We did some good things together, like playing basketball and baseball and listening to music. He was able to get me on to the Our Lady of the Snows basketball team when I did not even go to the school. He also encouraged me to get back into baseball and join him on his baseball team in the Pony League, and both were great, memorable experiences that I am thankful for. He was a good friend, and hanging around with him helped me (and maybe him), as we were going through the pains of growing up. It was a mix of activities and events with a friend who seemed at the time as troubled and rebellious as I was.

The last time I saw him was when we were around sixteen years old. I ran into him at a candy store on Union Turnpike, and we talked casually, shook hands, and said goodbye.

And I never saw him again.

We recently reconnected on Facebook, and I was happy to see that he has done very well in life. Our journeys took us down very different paths, yet somehow we are communicating again, and, after so many years, a bond remains that is difficult to explain.

September came around, and school started. Having skipped the eighth grade, I was now in ninth. The work was moving along at a rapid though reasonable pace when, in October, it was announced that there would be a teachers' strike. Suddenly, there was no school, though the general thinking was that the strike would be short-lived. That would not be the case, as the strike continued for two months until November 1968.

I spent most days with a good friend named Ari, who lived a block south of me. We played touch football outdoors in some cold weather, moved indoors to play a fantasy NFL football game, and smoked a bunch of cigarettes wherever we were. During what seemed like a never-ending period of time, it was announced and word spread that classes would be held in local synagogues and churches by our teachers. I thought it was some sort of joke and did not want to attend. However, my mother pushed me to go, so I did. I sat through one or two math classes given by a serious and mean teacher who seemed to take an immediate dislike to me, and the feeling was mutual.

I presumed that the material being covered in those classes would be reviewed when school resumed. In my mind it wasn't "real" school and we couldn't be held responsible, so I decided not to attend any additional classes. When the strike ended and we returned to school, that same teacher picked up where she had left off in those offsite classes, and there was no review of that material. As math is cumulative, not having learned what was covered previously and the speed and amount of material from combining two years into one left me totally lost.

Although math was never my best subject, up to that point, I could hold my own and grasp most of the material. Now, it was very uncomfortable to sit in the class, unable to comprehend the material. The teacher, whom I didn't like and had conflicts with, would embarrass me in front of my classmates by accusing me of not studying. I would answer back, and, as a result, things really deteriorated. I was always a fighter, standing up to the crazy attacks of my parents on my character and behavior. I was not about to take it from this generally acknowledged bitch of a teacher.

At that point, I was passing my other subjects, but the amount of work and time needed to devote to it was overwhelming. I was sick of it and felt like a failure.

Years later (and due to my own curiosity), I spoke to someone who was involved in the creation of an SP-type program in a nearby district. He told me that the criteria for entry into those programs would place students who were accepted into a small percentage of the entire world population. It was an eye-opener for me, as there I was, thinking I was a dumb kid. The reality hit me how that was so far from the truth. One of the major reasons I had struggled was due to the situation at home and how those things were adversely impacting my life. It's hard to concentrate on algebra being taught at a rapid pace when your home life is in constant turmoil.

After the first grades came in and I failed math (as expected), my father was called to school by one of the guidance counselors. The decision was made to remove me from the program and put me into the eighth grade, where I should have been in the first place. I was told of the decision before my parents were, and I never told them. I knew their reaction would not be good and would add to their list of all the horrible things about me. To my surprise, they said nothing after they found out. I was tremendously relieved to be in a normal class away from the nerds and the pressure of that program. I also felt I would have a better shot at making the basketball team being in my proper grade.

Mrs. Blum threw one last dagger at me before I was rid of her. No one had told me to report to a different math class, so I continued to attend hers. One day, she started yelling at me in front of the class, saying, "What are you still doing here? You don't belong in this class!"

I yelled back at her that "No one told me to report anywhere else!"

She was disgusted. She wrote a note, told me to leave, and to take the note to the office. She was an abusive, mean woman, and I was glad to be rid of her. I was already a victim of abuse at home, and facing it with her was something I would not tolerate. The whole episode contributed to my growing anger and disillusionment with the so-called "smart" people in and around my life. I then had to start over in another class and felt a great sense of relief, though I was also a bit nervous.

I approached the new classroom and took a look inside through the classroom door window before entering. I saw what looked like chaos. After I entered the room, everyone was talking while a mild-mannered, bearded science teacher was trying to teach. He was almost completely ignored by the students. I was thinking about the contrast at what I was seeing compared to the nerd classes in the SP program. In those classes, there was complete silence while the teachers were speaking.

I recognized Phil sitting in the back row and noticed an empty seat next to him. We had been on good terms, though, up to that point, we were not extremely close. I took that seat and he was extremely welcoming.

I met Phil when we were both ten years old. I was playing basketball and decided to take a break. While I was sitting on a bench, Phil walked in and sat down. We had both stolen a cigarette from our respective parents, and, while smoking, we began talking. I had no idea that the seemingly trivial decision of choosing to sit next to him would positively change and impact me for the rest of my life. Eventually, we became brothers.

Acceptance by others was especially important to me due to the lack thereof from my parents. A negative reaction from a girl when I first entered the new class stirred up the pain I was always subconsciously fighting. I did fairly well with girls throughout junior and senior high school, but I did not have a huge amount of confidence. When other guys were rejected by a girl, which was common at that age, they would laugh it off and move on to the next one. Any rejection I experienced felt like the end of the world. Oddly, there were several pretty girls interested in me although I was not interested in them. I really wanted to find someone who I could have a real relationship with. However, it seemed to elude me. Though I hated any form of rejection, I would subconsciously sabotage relationships with girls who liked me. I think it was mainly because my rejection was my comfort zone. It sounds crazy, but if a girl treated me well, it made me uncomfortable.

The new class in the grade I was supposed to be in was easy for me. The pace of learning slowed down to a reasonable level, and the work was a breeze after what I had come from. Phil and I became very close, and there were other kids in the class who I had known and interacted with previously, so all was going well. I was playing basketball for the church team, and, that summer, I played on a baseball team in the Pony League.

However, things at home continued to deteriorate. My parents' newest disciplinary measure was to throw me out of the house when they would get especially angry with me. This was starting to happen on a regular basis, as they were losing more control over me as I became a teenager. Thankfully, Phil and his family were there to help. They would let me sleep over when I had no place to go.

One time when I was kicked out of my house, Phil, I, and a few guys we knew from the night center at our school decided we would go drinking. Up to that point, I had only tasted a few beers, but this would be the first time I would drink liquor. The guys who invited us to participate in this adventure had purchased half-pint bottles of Seagrams® 7 whiskey for the event. We met up and then walked around the neighborhood on a very cold winter night, drinking it straight from the bottle. I really didn't like it, and I never developed a taste for alcohol the way many of my friends did. It still wound up being a memorable night of experimentation and hanging out with some good guys. Phil and I had a good time and spent hours just talking and maybe sneaking a few cigarettes in his basement before falling asleep that night.

Phil's house was like a place of refuge, and I felt like a member of the family. I got remarkably close to his parents, particularly his mother. I also loved watching Alabama football games on Saturday afternoons with Phil and his dad (Mr. M). His sister Laura, who was two years older than me, would hang out with us at times. The three of us would sit at the kitchen table drinking tea and smoking cigarettes, and we would talk for hours. Though it seemed like those were such simple things to do, the contrast with the chaos in my house made it extra enjoyable and meaningful for me. Their family wasn't perfect, but, compared to mine, they were the Cleavers.

During the summer when I was sixteen years old, I took a driver's education class at a school in Jamaica, Queens. After the early morning class, I would stop at Phil's before heading home. He was a late sleeper, so until he woke up, his mom, Mrs. M, would make me coffee and we would sit and talk for a long time. I could speak freely and openly with her, something I rarely did with my mother, who could not be trusted. On the rare occasions when I would confide in her, she would often throw things back in my face, so I stopped doing it. Mrs. M was a very loving and nurturing person, which I believe is what I was subconsciously craving.

Many years later, when I was an adult and had moved to Tampa, Florida, I wrote Mrs. M a letter. She kindly and thoughtfully responded with some wonderful and very meaningful words. She wrote about how much she missed those days when I would hang around the house, saying that they were some of the best days of her life. Sadly, she passed away shortly after she sent the letter.

Though they were not a perfect family, they were people (among others) who reached out to a kid who was suffering. By doing that, they helped save me from a wrong path or even worse. I have never forgotten them and never will.

The morning after our drunken escapade, I had to go home, which was part of the absurd game. After the devastation and rejection of being kicked out of my own house by my parents, they usually acted as if nothing ever happened. That was typical behavior on their part. After the beatings or being ripped to shreds verbally, my mother would act like an addict who had just had a fix. She would be calm and act like all was fine and had no concerns about or awareness of how those scars never fully heal.

What I have learned is that she and my father obviously had severe emotional problems. In that period of time, most people did not go for therapy or seek any sort of help. She had no control over her actions, and the shame of it was that other people liked her. She and my dad could both be very charming and sociable when they wanted to be and yet fighting a fight in the dark with no training. They had a good life and never appreciated it, which is the really sad part of the story.

I went home the next morning, and, after entering the house, I picked up the Sunday edition of the *Long Island Press*. I was reading the sports section when I noticed a good-sized photo of four other guys and me, including Phil. We had won the regional volleyball championship conducted by the night centers, and they took a picture of our team and did a small write-up describing the victory. It was a great feeling of accomplishment to win that, and seeing our picture in the widely read newspaper made it even more rewarding. I went from having a terrible experience to a great one overnight!

❧

Moving into the ninth grade, the decision for the school was to either break up the class or give us the toughest teachers available. They decided on the latter, and while the tough teachers really were tough, they couldn't break our spirit. It appears the way they obtained revenge was to screw us on our grades and possibly on our New York State Regents exams. We were warned about this by our science teacher in the eighth grade, that if we kept up our bad behavior, we would pay a price. We never listened to him about much of anything, so we pretty much ignored what he said. Reality would hit toward the end of the ninth grade school year when we took the Regents exams.

The teachers in our ninth-grade classes were very tough, which we learned was the plan for how to deal with our class from the previous year. The kids in our class were mostly smart though not inclined toward school as a top priority like the SP kids were. The classes were the next tier below the SPs and included learning a foreign language.

Basically, we were a bunch of smart kids who were wiseasses. I would later learn while in the business world that those were the same characteristics shared by some of the most successful people I ever worked with.

The combination of tough teachers and wiseass students led to several confrontations and mistrust on both sides.

The junior-high grand finale was yet to take place. Some of my grades had gone down in the third quarter, and the big one was math. I went from a 90 in the second quarter to a 65 in the third for no apparent reason. Rather than hear it from my parents, I came up with a better idea.

The process was that you had a parent sign the report card in the designated area. I decided that I would ask my friend John to forge my mother's signature. He did a few practice runs and was incredibly good at it, so I decided to go ahead and turn it in. Though it passed scrutiny at the time, the problem was that my mother noticed it when I gave her the final report card at the end of the school year. She was really pissed off and told me, "When your father gets home he's going to play ball with your head."

I wasn't really looking forward to that, so I took a walk to the park on the corner to think about the upcoming head bouncing. Running away crossed my mind, which was something I had thought about from time to time over the years.

When I got to the park, I ran into my friend Dan, who I had not seen in a while. He asked me how I was doing, and I told him, "I think I have to run away."

After I explained why, he told me he had run away three days prior and had not been home since. We both laughed hysterically!

I was wearing a button-down shirt over a T-shirt and Dan sported just a tee. He asked if he could borrow my top shirt to avoid being detected by his father, who had been looking for him. He then began to explain a plan he had for the runaway.

The first step would be to take a short walk to the Glen Oaks Apartments where two other guys were waiting. I loaned him the shirt, and, as we left the park and walked across 80th Avenue, a car suddenly pulled up and screeched to a halt. To our surprise, his father flew out of the car and was very angry. He glared at Dan and shouted, "What's the matter with you?"

Dan replied, "Nothing, what's the matter with you?"

This went back and forth several times, and then his father got back in the car and took off. We were nearly rolling on the floor, laughing our asses off.

We proceeded to meet the other guys, Jared and Joe, who were waiting for us in the back of the apartment where Joe lived. He was the one with the car, and the plan was to drive upstate where his uncle had a farm. We would stay there for the summer and work for our keep. A few boys just turning fifteen were more than ready to hit the road.

We waited for quite a while until it became apparent that Joe would not break free that night. With nowhere to go and midnight approaching, we found an abandoned car that became our place to sleep for the night. I didn't sleep at all—just tossed and turned until daylight.

When we woke, we were hungry and decided to take a walk down Union Turnpike to Sol's candy store/luncheonette and were able to have a decent breakfast. After the meal, we started to walk back to where Joe lived in hopes of him being able to proceed with the plan.

We made it two blocks when a car pulled up next to us, and out came Dan's father. This time he wasn't messing around. He demanded that Dan get into the car, which he did.

Now Jared and I were the only ones left, so we decided that we would go to Dan's house in New Hyde Park. To prevent our parents from finding us, we took a path through an area by Long Island Jewish Hospital, fighting our way through some woods and climbing a number of fences.

When we made it through that back-road path, we were filthy, with mud all over our clothes and a few cuts on our arms. We did not know what to expect at Dan's house, thinking maybe he would rejoin us. As we approached the house, he came walking down the street toward us, all cleaned up and showered and smoking a Marlboro. He told us there were no repercussions from his parents regarding the adventure.

It then hit me that perhaps this was not a good plan after all, so I had to figure out how to get out of the messy situation. At the time, I hadn't realized the survivalist skills I had developed. I had already faced years of abuse at the hands of those who were supposed to be my guides and protectors and love me unconditionally. Surviving those years and fighting back would prepare me not only for surviving the streets and tough teen years but also for adult life with all its challenges. I was left with skills and an inner strength that would serve me very well in what the future would hold.

My conclusion was that I had to call home. I went to a local phone booth, made the call, and my father answered. He was sort of apologetic and tried to convince me to come home. He explained how they were trying to be good parents, so, without any alternatives, I agreed to return home.

I don't believe that he was a bad person, and he probably was trying. He had a great personality and related well to people. That was confirmed years later when I reconciled with my aunt, who was his sister. She told me that when he was young, all the people in their Coney Island neighborhood loved him. She was baffled at how much he changed after he met my mother and eventually cut off his own family. It became apparent that, in his own way, he was also a victim of my mother's illnesses. Eventually, he became like her, in a symbiotic relationship pitting them against the entire world, including their children.

It was a major disappointment that the father who came to my defense against the neighbor who hit me when I was a child would never defend me against my mother and her violent attacks on my sister and me. Because of that, I have no respect for him, only pity.

For me, junior high was a mixed bag on steroids. After all that transpired, both good and bad, I carried a tremendous amount of resentment toward the authority of my parents and some of the teachers. I also resented many (though not all) of the Jewish kids who remained in the SP program and especially the basketball coach who cut me from the team while it was well-known and acknowledged that he screwed me. The disappointing conclusion of my relationship with Cynthia and finally how it ended with Amy also rankled deep in my heart.

I had hoped that somewhere down the road, Amy and I would meet up again, as we were so young when we had our brief relationship. It was a pipe dream, a fantasy that provided me with an escape from the realities I was facing at the time. It was the night the New York Knicks, a team I felt so close to from the camp experience, the team I loved more than any other, won the NBA Championship. I had made out with a very pretty girl at a church carnival, but it made me think of Amy. I decided that I would call her, as the chance of reconnecting, if even as friends, outweighed my fear of the possibility of rejection.

I went to the local candy-store phone booth, dropped in the coin, and dialed. Her sister answered and was friendly when I asked to speak to Amy. She returned to say that Amy did not want to talk to me, which was a surprise. I took the walk home feeling a mix of emotions from the joy of the Knicks championship to the rejection from the girl of my dreams (at least at the time) all swirling through my mind. It was a mixed bag of an evening concluding the mixed bag of my junior high years.

As a result of those experiences, I developed a point of view that somehow combined it all into one big dilemma. In my mind, the teachers, Amy, the SP nerds, friends who made the basketball team knowing I was better than them, and my parents all became one world of rejection. My attitude was that if you all reject me, I will reject you and your world.

I ultimately learned that was not a totally correct perception, though it was what I strongly believed at that time. That perception led to what would become, putting it mildly, a very wild three years that followed. The next stop on the journey would be high school, carrying the pain and weight of what had already transpired while celebrating only my fifteenth birthday. I rejected their world and would now enter an entirely new one.

CHAPTER 8

New Roads:
Smooth and Rough

*T*hings were relatively quiet during the summer prior to entering Martin Van Buren High School. Several of us guys who were too young to "officially" work (other than having a paper route) found out we could make some money caddying.

The Glen Oaks Country Club was located just north of our neighborhood. Its members were mostly doctors, lawyers, and other professionals who had money. Several of the kids from our neighborhood and the surrounding ones would all congregate and wait in the "caddy yard" hoping to be selected by the "caddy master" that would bring the good fortune of going out on a "loop."

The loop could include two to four players and carrying zero to two bags on your back for 18 holes. The caddy was responsible for finding the golf ball after the (mostly bad) golfers would hit them, handing the golfers the clubs they requested, and washing the clubs at the end of the round. Doing this could earn you between $12 to $18 for the grueling work.

We would sometimes spend hours hanging around in the caddy yard, waiting to be selected or realizing we would not be chosen that day. The time hanging out with all the guys made for some interesting and hysterically funny incidents. I could say that the events in the movie *Caddyshack* were not far from what we experienced there. It made the waiting time more tolerable and fun.

That camaraderie with the guys was so important in helping me cope with the pain of things happening at home. It was only a brief time in our teen years; however, the stories from that experience live on and are still being told to this day.

❧

Summer dragged on and spending time with my friend John's older brother Nick was special. He was somewhat of a role model to John, Johnny, Phil, and me. We looked up to him, as he was a few years older and a "cool" guy. In a way, he was like an older brother to all of us. He would drive us around while playing music we had never really listened to. Crosby Stills and Nash (CS&N), Neil Young, and the Grateful Dead were some of the bands I had not paid close attention to up to that point. We were also introduced to weed, and while that was new, it was not anything out of the ordinary at that time as it was spreading all around the neighborhood. I had some conflicted, guilty feelings smoking weed, as I would remember my grandmother saying to me while she would be washing dishes in her kitchen to promise her I would never do drugs. She instilled a conscience in me that I did not see or detect in others around me.

September rolled around, and suddenly it was our last Friday before entering a new world that we were not looking forward to. On Monday, the bus on Hillside Avenue pulled up in front of this building with a big clock on the face of it. It was all strange and new at first, though, after a while, I adjusted. I was placed in a French language class, geometry for my math class, and biology for my science requirement. The school had a very good reputation at that time and the makings of a good education were there for those who wanted it. The number of students who went on to become doctors, lawyers, businesspeople, and other professionals was impressive. On the other side of the coin were the wilder kids who had other priorities and attended just because they had to. At that point in time, I was among the latter.

Deep inside, I still had some small hope that maybe a few of my earlier goals from junior high could be achieved and my shattered dreams could be fulfilled. Despite my parents' abuse and the resulting trauma that I had to endure, I still had belief in myself. My ego was strong, which I believe my grandmother had instilled in me from when I was a baby living in her house and during our relationship through to my early teens. Yet it was a constant battle of that self-belief and hope against the persistent verbal sadism and abuse my mother directed at me.

The dream of playing on the Van Buren basketball team that I had a few years earlier was a long shot at that point.

One day, they announced tryouts for the JV team would be held after school in the gym. The coach of the JV and varsity teams was a heralded, knowledgeable man who had led teams to New York City Championship games. He would arrange five guys on a side and send them out for a short scrimmage. He then would point to one or two guys and tell them to stay, and the others could pack up and go home.

Though I had not played competitively for over a year and lost confidence in my game, I decided to give it a try. I got off one shot and missed and, not to my surprise, was sent home. Ironically, the only guy from junior high to make it was a tall, lanky guy who was one of the three that was cut from that team along with me.

That was the final nail in the dreams and world I knew two years prior, and I had no idea where things would go from there.

CHAPTER 9

The Big I

I rang the bell on Phil's front door, and, when his mother opened it, she told me that Phil had already gone out. I asked which direction he had gone, and she pointed south toward Hillside Avenue. He and I were both searching for somewhere to hang our hats, so to speak. We wondered which group in the neighborhood we should start hanging around with.

Always looking for a new adventure, I decided I would go to Hillside Avenue. I ran into Phil and a small group in front of Carmine's house.

Carmine was a guy I knew from school and our flag football team. Up to that time, I hadn't associated with him outside of those two activities. I also recognized the Donahue twin brothers, Mike and Vic, from the church basketball team. They were from a large Irish family and had two older brothers, Joe and Paul; twin sisters, Marge and Dianne; and a sister named Chloe. The older brother, Paul, would eventually be nicknamed "HT."

As I came walking up to them, they greeted me with, "Hey, look who's here . . ."

We were off and running! I began my membership as the only Jew (though I could pass for Italian or Spanish) among the twenty or so Irish and Italian guys. The name they gave themselves was the "Big I," standing for Irish and Italian, though eventually they threw in Israel for my benefit. I was accepted and had found a new home.

We were like the guys in a TV show called *The Bowery Boys,* which was about a group of wise-guy city kids that would hang out and get into all sorts of mischief. We weren't an official gang, but it was like we were. If you fought one of us, you fought all, and we had a reputation as guys that were not to be messed with.

We mostly hung out on Hillside Avenue and 259th Street in what would be described as an old-fashioned candy store. It was a great place to hang out, especially during the cold New York winters. We were well behaved, as the owners were well respected and had some tough family members who we knew you did not want to offend.

Next to this store was a bar called "Herman's Tavern," an old-man's bar where we could hang out on weekend nights because the bartender would let us in even though we ranged in age from fifteen to seventeen.

Most people today would consider that to be criminal; however, I found that in my case it was a great learning experience.

One Saturday night when we were in there, I looked at the old men sitting at the bar drinking their hard liquor. As problematic as things were in my family, my father never did that type of thing, ever! I thought how I didn't ever want to wind up like those men, sitting in a bar alone on a Saturday night, and, thankfully, I never did. I realized sometimes it's better to let kids learn their own lessons by seeing and experiencing the real world instead of sheltering them from it.

As time went by, this group of guys grew into a brotherhood. Though we didn't realize or weren't conscious of it at the time, each of us seemed to have family issues that drove us to each other as a family substitute. That's the attraction of gangs. Some of the guys had lost either a father or mother at an early age; one father was emotionally damaged from WWII. Other parents were alcoholics and/or abusive.

From the beginning, I felt accepted by those guys for who I was without conditions. That's what a family should be for each other, and mine wasn't. Even later in life, when people were going to reunions and reconnecting, this group rarely, if ever, even asked what I was doing career-wise. When I went to my high school and other reunions, that was the first thing people asked. It was a stark contrast between the way people assessed me and each other. The Big I guys could care less what I was doing: they were just happy to see me.

Carmine was among the toughest in the group. His father had fought in WWII and the story was that his jeep was hit, and, as a result, he never would drive again. Carmine had a lot of anger and would take it out on others at times. He wasn't a big guy, but he wasn't afraid to fight anyone . . . and, most of the time, he would win. He took a liking to me and we became good friends throughout high school.

One night we wound up in a bar on Union Turnpike that was a little bit out of our turf, but we knew some of the guys there and did not expect any trouble. Carmine and some guy got into a dispute, one word led to another, and they agreed to take it outside. The other guy was pretty big, but I knew how Carmine could fight.

We all went outside, and I was the only guy there to step in if needed, as the other guy had five or six friends there. I had to be ready to go and help my friend if any of the other guy's friends jumped in. That was the brotherhood/family law of the street in those days.

The two of them went at it for a while, rolling around on the ground. I was surprised the other guy was hanging in for that long, but I remained on high alert the whole time, ready to go at it if it was called for. Finally, they agreed to call it a draw and everyone walked away. As wild as Carmine was, I could always reason with him and talked him out of kicking a few guys' asses, guys I knew from my earlier days. And he always had my back!

I continued to hang out with the Big I during my sophomore year in high school. That June, I turned sixteen, which was a major milestone. My grandmother had a bad stroke and was in the hospital, and I didn't know exactly what that meant. My mother did not want me to go to the hospital and she didn't tell me how severe it was. I knew old people got sick, but I didn't think it would be that bad.

The day arrived when my grandmother would be released from the hospital. My mother decided she would take care of her at our house, and my grandfather would come out from Brooklyn to visit a few times a week. She arrived at our house, and I came downstairs expecting to see Grandma as I knew her, just sitting in a wheelchair. I was shocked at what I saw. She was in the wheelchair, but the side of her face had dropped, and she was crying nonstop. My grandma, who diligently tended to her little garden and roses and played catch with me when I was bored, the one who loved and protected me from the time I was born, was not the same anymore. I walked up the steps to my room and thought, *Now this on top of everything else.*

I was shattered.

Feeling depressed and growing tired of the same old things, I needed a change. So I decided to seek something new. I was also both maturing and becoming more rebellious, which is typical of teen behavior. However, as my parents were losing more control, their abuse became worse. Normal teen rebellion was seen as some big challenge to them and their control, which led to many confrontations. I would yell back and curse them but never physically fight back. I decided at one point to let my mother flail away and just take it as if it had no physical effect on me. The longer I showed no reaction, the more powerful and vicious her blows became. The verbal abuse was also worsening. They would call my sister and me crazy and threaten that they were going to commit us to a mental institution. They even made my sister pack her bags one time when she was only thirteen years old. The pressure of my grandmother's illness was impacting us all, but it mostly affected my mother. That also contributed to the escalation of her abuse. As bad as the situation had been, it was deteriorating even more as the summer began.

Though it could not be officially diagnosed second-hand, my therapist believed that based on everything I told him, my mother was suffering from borderline personality disorder. This very much explained what I had seen and experienced from her. The emotional dysregulation, unstable relationships, unstable self-image, intense mood swings, and explosive anger are a few of the traits that registered with me regarding her illness. Books have been written about children raised by such parents.

In the book *Surviving A Borderline Parent*, the first chapter is entitled "I Never Knew It Had a Name."[2] A blogger once wrote, "If this is your parent, the first and best thing you can do is head for the hills."

Similarly, in an online article "The Borderline Personality Disordered Family, Part II: The Children," Allan Schwartz, LCSW, PhD wrote that one of the factors regarding what saves some survivors of the abuse is running away from home. The writer states, "There are those children who run away from home. For most children this is not a good idea because they can fall into the hands of predators in the outside world. However, I have worked with a number of cases, where, once the child reached adolescence, they ran to the home of a friend and family they knew well and found permanent protection."[3]

In adulthood, learning about this illness was very helpful. I pity my mother, who suffered from it her whole life. Toward the end, she did realize many related things and also the amount of damage it did to her children and others.

What helped me cope with the pain of my grandmother's situation was when I took a part-time summer job working three hours a day in a luncheonette deli owned by a friend's father, located in the town of Great Neck, a few miles northeast from my house. I would hitch rides both ways every day to work as a dishwasher, and, for three hours of work, I would get a free sandwich and have a few dollars for spending money that night.

My evenings would start with the purchase of a half pint of vodka to drink in the park next to JHS 172 where a few attractive girls hung out. I needed a change from Hillside and this was a place I tried out. I played handball and got to know some of the girls.

There was also an older group of guys and girls who hung out in another area of the park. Some were three to five years older than me, but somehow I gradually started to hang out with them.

At first, I would test the waters by sitting on the bench where they would gather, hoping not to get told to get lost or, worse, get my ass kicked. They were tough, and some were bullies, really mean guys who would think nothing of beating the shit out of a younger guy. But I figured, hey, if my parents say I'm crazy, I will show them what crazy really was.

The leader of the older guys was a guy they called "Big Daddy." He had a purple Harley and a '63 Chevy with no back seat. He was a big strapping guy, around 6'5" tall with a goatee and long hair combed back '50s style. He also had a tattoo of a devil lady on his arm. For some reason, he took a liking to me, and, as time went on, I hung out with him quite a bit. This was a whole new downward level for me to be hanging out with this guy and that group of people.

He was also the guy who would bring different drugs to the park and either sell them or just give them out.

One night, shortly before my move to hang out with them, Phil and I were sitting in the handball courts. Big Daddy was standing there smoking a joint when he said to someone else to "pass it to the younger degenerates," meaning me and Phil. We were honored that he included us.

One night, it would be weed; another, downs or ups; and then the big one: LSD. It was the infamous "Orange Sunshine," and I decided I would try it. I figured, how bad could it be? I'd try anything once. I told Big Daddy of my intentions and he was happy to accommodate. The "tab" was tiny, like the tip of a match, and orange colored. I took it and let it dissolve a little bit before swallowing it. Then we sat around for quite a while. Nothing seemed to be happening. The guys kept asking if I felt anything, and I became impatient, so I asked for more. I bit off around another half a tab and continued to wait for something to kick in.

A short while later, it kicked in . . . and it was like going into another world. I thought I saw one of the guys, Tino, walking outside the park. The older guys, who couldn't be trusted, said, "Yeah, that's him!" so I walked outside the park. The guy I thought was Tino was walking his dog.

I called out to him in a questioning way, "Tino? Tino?" really thinking it was him. When I got near him, I realized it wasn't Tino, just some poor guy walking his dog. I freaked and started yelling at him, "You're not Tino!" The guy got scared and took off with his dog.

I tried to drink some beer and it tasted like blood. At one point someone said, "The pigs are here," and I thought it was a joke. On that type of LSD, it was hard to determine reality from fantasy. I realized it was real when I heard the cop's voice telling us to get out of the park. I complied, and, while I was walking past him, I saw the cop in police uniform with the head of the cartoon character Porky Pig.

After getting kicked out of the park, we promptly jumped into Big Daddy's car. I was sitting in the front seat and he threw an 8-track tape into the deck of the Jimi Hendrix song "Power of Soul." The lyrics were crazy, as it was from a live performance given by Jimi, and it wasn't very helpful in my state of mind.

We reached our destination, which was a bar on Hillside Avenue called George's, and, inside, it was really weird but tolerable. After hanging out there a while, we decided we could go back to the park.

We arrived there and were just mulling around. Big Daddy messed with me by showing me the tattoo of the devil lady on his forearm, telling me that she was the one who had given him the acid. Suddenly, his girlfriend and some of her friends pulled up in a car and came to where we were hanging out. She said to Big Daddy, "Come on, let's get out of here and away from these kids."

She meant me, and when you are on acid, hearing something like that really affects you deeply. The departure of the original group of people who were part of the trip was very upsetting. They left, and now I was on my own.

It was getting late, and I started to walk home. As I was making my way, I remembered someone once said, "You see rats when you're tripping."

I looked over at what was probably a pile of beer cans and, sure enough, I saw a group of rats.

When I finally arrived home, I wasn't sure what to do. I stood looking at my house and wondering what would happen if my father started yelling at me for some reason. How would I react? Would I scream like I did earlier in the bar? The one alternative was to go to Hillside, but the guys there were probably drunk, and that would not be a good match for my state of mind.

Running out of options, I looked again at my house, and, through the front living room window, I could see my father sitting there smoking a cigarette. I decided I had to face whatever might happen but that I had to go inside.

I slipped in the key and opened the door to find no one sitting there; it was another hallucination. I promptly went upstairs to my room hoping my kid brother was sleeping downstairs, which he often did in the summertime. My parents had the only air conditioner in the house, and, on hot nights, he would sleep on the floor in their room.

I looked over at the other bed and saw what looked like a burnt pygmy. It was my brother! I turned away very quickly and was ready for the second leg of the journey.

I lie in bed all night, never able to sleep. Layers of assorted colors spun round and round, forming different shapes and figures. Broken lines composed each image I saw. One moment, I would see a bumblebee and focus on it. I seemed to be diving into it, and then a new image would emerge . . . and all this was happening in constant motion. I would see these images whether my eyes were closed and open. It didn't matter.

I also had what could be described as auditory hallucinations, like hearing sounds like a locomotive engine or sirens from fire trucks or ambulances. I would imagine myself walking down Union Turnpike, and then I was unable to differentiate where I really was: in my bed or walking down the street. This went on all night and into the next morning as the effects of the trip gradually subsided. As night transformed to daylight, I could still see the spinning colors, steadily fading away.

The trip also produced several deep thoughts related to the experience, both during and shortly afterward. I thought that I had obtained an understanding of what people like Jimi Hendrix and John Lennon were all about. I had now entered some new sort of brotherhood in which we all shared a unique experience. It was like my eyes were opened, and, although it was an exhausting and wild experience, I liked it. I experimented with a few different drugs that summer and for a while beyond, but tripping was always an adventure, and it became my experiment of choice for the next two years.

The adventures were not always good, as I found out the second time around. Despite my drift away from the Hillside guys to the 172 Boys, I maintained my friendship with Phil, John, and Johnny. Some nights that summer, we would just hang out in front of Phil or John's house and play some touch football with John's older brother.

Nick became like an older brother figure to me. He was one of the 172 Boys, and that summer he and two of his friends bought a car from a police auction and spent the summer going cross-country. That experience changed all of them. They became very anti-New York, stopped hanging around with the more violent people at the park, and, in general, became more introspective. They just wanted to smoke some weed and listen to good music. The previous summer, Nick would drive us around and turn us on to some great music. The first CS&N album became a favorite along with Jethro Tull's *Aqualung*, Traffic's *John Barleycorn*, Leon Russell, Ten Years After, and a few others.

I saw Nick when he returned from his cross-country journey, which was shortly after my first acid trip. He threw on the Grateful Dead's latest work *American Beauty*. It was one of their studio albums, and I thought it was fantastic.

Listening to CS&N brought me more into an acoustic realm that was quite different from Hendrix and the other harder-edged music that I had been into. The songs were poetry in motion, deep into the human experience. The songs with lyrics from the pen of Robert Hunter, songwriter of the Grateful Dead, impacted me the most. Their music went hand in hand with the acid and could take you on some amazing journeys.

One night, after some touch football with Nick, Phil, and a few others, the discussion shifted to tripping. Phil expressed his desire to do it, and I warned him, as did Nick, but warning Phil was like egging him on.

It turned out that Nick had some Sunshine in his house, which he brought out to us. Phil did some, and I decided to join in. I was so concerned about Phil that the acid didn't seem to hit me until I got home around midnight. Phil had to be assisted, so I focused on that as he worked his way through.

When I got home and it started to hit me, I realized I was having what was called a "bad trip." My mind was consumed with sad thoughts about my grandmother, what had transpired with Amy, and other disturbing things. At the time, I did not realize how those two things were emotionally connected. Both were times in my life that at one point were extremely good and then turned extremely bad. When in that state of mind with everything accentuated, those thoughts were extremely depressing.

As the summer wore on, I began hanging around with a lowlife named Micky. He had a tough family life and was troubled, to say the least. Before I got to know him, I and a few other friends looked up to him. He was a big guy with a full beard and looked very intimidating. When we got to know him, he could be very witty and funny, but he also had a very dark side.

Even though I hung out with him quite a bit, I never really trusted him. He was a bad influence on me and not a good guy, and being friends with him was a new low for me. But that period of time made me realize that the downward path I was on was not what I wanted or who I really was.

The tumultuous, life changing, and traumatic summer I had led to my decision to tone it all down, focus more on school, and look for some new friends and experiences. My mother had sent my grandmother home to Brooklyn, as she couldn't handle caring for her. It was hard to understand that she was sending her mother, whom she claimed to love so much, back to live with my grandfather, the man she hated and would constantly vilify.

My mother's abusive actions came to a head one day, and I determined that I had had enough. It was December and the holiday season, so I decided I would try to get a full-time job so I could quit school and move out. I felt like I had no choice, and the first step was to find a job.

I went to a nearby department store called S. Klein's that I heard was hiring. They hired me as a temp for the Christmas season, to be a porter. I was thrilled to have my first real job, and a new adventure was about to unfold.

CHAPTER 10

Whirlwind

*T*he Hillside guys were changing from leather jackets and Marlboros to more of what was reflective of the times. They were smoking pot regularly and several had also tried acid. The music was now mostly Grateful Dead focused, though Allman Brothers, Hot Tuna, and The Doors were gaining popularity with the group. Some of the guys were now seventeen years old and had obtained driver's licenses, which opened new doors like local clubs to meet girls. There were also the beginnings of a movement from the street corners to a place nearby known as Alley Pond Park. At Alley Pond Park there was a big parking lot on the upper level in which cars would park to party and listen to music. Later in the evening, it would turn into more of a "lovers' lane," where couples could do their thing.

John, who lived next door to Phil, had gone off to college at the University of Buffalo, and Phil was starting to hang out with a subgroup within the Hillside Guys that was moving more toward the club scene. I was sad that two of my closest friends and I were moving in different directions.

However, the job at Klein's brought me into a whole new world. It was holiday season, and the store was bustling and full of energy.

As a porter, my job involved walking a pushcart around the store to each department and emptying their trash into a receptacle on my cart. It was easy and allowed me to get to know people in each department. I was a bit naive as to how much partying was going on with the workers in the store, as one guy informed me that if I wanted acid, the guy playing Santa Claus had it, and that you could get pot from the hardware manager, and so on. It was a pretty wild scene, reflective of the times.

I was beginning to find a new path, and it started with me hanging out with some of the people from work after hours. Some of them would hang around at a bar at a Chinese restaurant called Wayne Wong's that was located in the Lake Success Shopping Center where Klein's was. I was able to help my friend Carmine get a job in the restaurant within Klein's, and he would also join in with the new group at Wayne Wong's. I still hung around Hillside quite a bit and at Hogan's bar, but I wanted and needed a change.

The break room in Klein's was where workers could grab a coffee, have a smoke, and, if needed, use the phone booth located there. One day, a woman who I recognized worked in the Women's Accessories department sat down with me at my table. She seemed nice, and any time we wound up on our breaks at the same time, she would join me at a table and we would talk.

One of those times, she sat down and started to cry, so I asked her what was wrong. She told me that some people had treated her badly and said some mean things that were very upsetting. I tried to cheer her up and brought up her artwork just to make conversation. I told her that I would like to see it sometime, not thinking that would ever happen. She said that would be great and asked if I would like to come to her apartment that Friday night. Though I was a bit surprised, I said I would let her know.

Her name was Pam, and she was attractive, although not my dream girl. I wasn't sure what to make of the situation since she was twice my age, so I took it to Phil so we could analyze it and decide what I should do. Sitting at his kitchen table, we concluded that she was either going to murder me or that I was going to get laid. After some back and forth, I decided that I would go.

The pretty girl I had made out with a year earlier at a local carnival lived near to where I thought Pam's apartment was located in Glen Oaks. Phil jokingly said, "Just make sure you don't run into Martha on the way to that woman's apartment!"

When I told Pam it was a go, she asked if it would be okay if another couple joined us. That freaked me out, and I told her I wasn't into that, and she said that was fine and that it would just be the two of us.

It was a cold January night, and my first stop was at the liquor store on Union Turnpike to pick up a pint of vodka. I also had four joints with me and thought that would get us through the evening. I made my way walking up 260th Street and arrived at what I thought was her apartment. I rang the bell, and who answered the door but Martha, the real pretty girl I was determined to avoid. I couldn't believe it! I knew I had to think fast. She was surprised and politely asked what I was doing there. I apologized and said I was looking for my aunt's place. I was embarrassed, but I ultimately laughed it off as it was one of those "You can't make this shit up" moments.

I turned the corner and found the right apartment, and Pam came down to answer the door. She was wearing a polo shirt and striped pants. She made me a screwdriver and told me she didn't drink or smoke pot. Her record collection was limited regarding anything I liked, though I noticed there was an album of The Band. Their song "The Weight" was playing when she asked me to help her get up from the sofa. When I reached to help her, she pulled me down on top of her.

I went back one more time after that very wild night and realized I didn't want the relationship to continue. Though it was fun and enjoyable in a way, I realized it wasn't what I really wanted. I longed for a relationship with the right girl, and this certainly wasn't that. I felt bad for her, but I left and made known that our relationship would not continue. It was a very strange yet unforgettable experience for a sixteen-year-old.

స్

From a certain perspective, I was having a pretty good time working at Klein's. However, when you are the victim of child abuse—physical, verbal, and psychological—it impacts you in ways you don't understand at the time. It wasn't until many years later that I developed enough of an understanding to begin to work through it all. Self-esteem gets destroyed, and, at a certain point, you withdraw from abusive parents and start believing the terrible things they say to you about yourself.

It hit me how certain experiences were directly related to the abuse, particularly the verbal and psychological. My mother would often insult mine and my sisters' looks and weight. "Look at you, you fat, ugly black thing" is an example of the sadistic and vicious things she would say to me. She would say similar things to my sister and younger brother.

Most children go through various awkward stages in which they are extremely self-conscious, and hearing abusive insults from those who are supposed to be loving and nurturing is devastating. You start believing it and your self-worth becomes severely damaged. Even much later in life, when someone tries to be funny and makes a negative remark about my looks, it can be like a dagger going through my heart.

The failure in Little League at a young age made me not want my father to attend the games. I also did not invite either parent to the championship game at basketball camp. At the time I did not understand why; I just knew that I did not want them there. My mother would often throw in comparisons to other children into her negative assessments of us: "Look how Ron across the street helps his father all the time. You don't lift a finger to help. They all were going to quit Hebrew school, only you did. They were all going to get kicked out of the SP, and only you did."

I learned that after experiencing that type of verbal abuse, a child withdraws from his/her parent(s). The fear of further disappointing the parent if they don't excel in things like sports or music can become extreme.

Subconsciously, that is what I did, and when my grandfather criticized my guitar playing at the age of eleven, it had me believing that I was an ugly failure. I gave up on the things I loved most and quit doing them. The resentment and anger had steadily built up and led me to do things that were out of character with who I really was. But I never forgot my grandmother, aunts, and uncles and the love given to me in that house in Brooklyn during the early years of my life. I believe those family members and their love were major factors in my eventual recovery.

My career at Klein's ended abruptly after I had a fist-fight with the hardware manager. We exchanged words over the removal of a skid from the basement freight elevator that I was ordered to remove by my boss. The manager would not let me remove it because he was trying to bring some merchandise to a customer waiting on the first floor. I let him go, and my boss called down on an internal phone yelling at me to "get that thing off the elevator immediately."

The hardware manager somehow missed the first floor and wound up back at the basement level. I told him I had to get the skid off now and he refused. It got heated, and as

I walked away, I noticed a handcart. I grabbed it and threw it at him.

He came at me and I responded, hitting him several times until he went down. I had him in a headlock, and a few women who were ticketing items near us were screaming hysterically. The toy department manager came in, and he and others pulled me off him. A few days later, I was called into the executive manager's office to tell my story of what happened.

We were both fired a week later.

Things were changing, and it was a lonely time. John had gone off to college in Buffalo; Phil had a girlfriend and was starting to hang out with a different crowd who all had steady girlfriends. That crowd would often meet up later in the night after spending time with their girls and go to some of the local clubs. I would join them sometimes, but it was not really my thing.

I started to hang around with a girl named Tina who had also worked at Klein's. She was attractive and a little older than I was. We were just friends, and I enjoyed hanging out with her, just listening to Grateful Dead music and talking. One night, we suddenly kissed, and it was one of those magical moments. We wound up sleeping together once, but our friendship continued (though, for her, I was a friend and one of many other guys).

It disturbed me a little, though I knew it was not going to be any sort of lasting relationship. I still had that thing where I wanted to be the only guy, though I knew that would not be the case with this girl. We liked each other as friends and always would.

The Beatles had already broken up, and each of the former members were out on their own. Like many others, I enjoyed the music from each of them, though I took a particular liking to George Harrison's work. He was the "quiet Beatle," and there was something intriguing about him.

I had heard about the Concert for Bangladesh, in which George put together what was believed to be the first mega rock concert for a charitable cause. There had been devastation in Bangladesh due to major rains and flooding. That created a humanitarian crisis, and the proceeds from the concert would be used to help aid the people of the fledgling country. The concert took place in August 1971 at Madison Square Garden in New York City, and the movie was released in 1972.

My good friend John was home on a break from college, and the movie was playing at the local Glen Oaks movie theater. We decided to go see it, and I foolishly thought it would be a good idea to drop some acid beforehand.

Though that action may have been foolish, it set off a series of events that led to some of the most dramatic changes of my entire life. I never could have imagined how going to see a movie of a concert would do that, let alone the fact that George Harrison would be the person to have such an impact on my life as he did.

The first musical guest was Ravi Shankar, an Indian sitarist, with fellow musicians who played music very foreign to me. I didn't like it. I was in awe of how fast the percussion players were playing what looked like some type of bongos. In the state I was in, I wasn't sure if they were really playing that fast or if I was imagining it. I asked John, and he confirmed they were playing extremely fast. But I was greatly relieved when they finished their segment.

Out came George, sporting a long beard, wearing a bright red shirt, and either a white suit or sport jacket. He was his mellow self, though he was very interactive with the audience. Here was the quiet Beatle like a master of ceremonies, speaking to the audience and introducing guests. He was the man in charge, and it was great to see him like that.

His friends who performed were an all-star list: Eric Clapton, Leon Russell, Billy Preston, Ringo, and Bob Dylan, and the music was fantastic.

I was never a huge fan of Bob Dylan's singing, though I liked several songs he wrote when performed by other artists. When George introduced him, it brought me down, thinking how bad it was going to be. To my pleasant surprise, he sang around five songs that took me into another world. I was drawn into the stories being told by the lyrics, and it was quite amazing.

As I sat there absorbing the music in my altered state of consciousness, I noticed an interesting pattern: many of the songs mentioned a spiritual connection. "Awaiting On You All," "That's the Way God Planned It," and "My Sweet Lord" all piqued my curiosity, and I began to wonder about what they were singing.

On the way home, John and I passed by Our Lady of the Snows church, and we stopped to look at the cross. I asked John, who was Catholic, what that was all about. He provided a brief explanation based on his religious training. The seed was planted, and a new spiritual journey would begin a short time later that changed my life in a major way.

My seventeenth birthday brought me that special moment of receiving my driver's license, and I purchased my first car. It was a '63 Chevy Super Sport whose previous owner had converted the transmission from a four speed to an automatic on the floor. It was a decent car, and I enjoyed finally having one, though, as I had suspected, the fantasy of how great life would become when we all had cars was not becoming a reality.

I had been away from Big Daddy and the older guys for several months when I went out with the new car for my first few drives, mostly around the neighborhood. My friends and I still had a fear of running into some of the older guys, as you never knew what they would do to you.

On one of the first nights, while riding around with John and Johnny, we discussed how bad it would be if we did encounter one of the older bullies. And then, like clockwork, one of those guys who I knew from the park (his name was Tino), spotted us. He waved at us and shouted, "Yo, I need a ride."

I knew that I needed to comply, so I pulled over. He said he needed a ride to pick up his paycheck. Sounded reasonable, so I asked, "Where?"

He said, "Brooklyn."

I was definitely not thrilled to do that, but I had no real choice. I let John and Johnny out of the car, and off Tino and I went, heading down 81st Avenue toward the Cross Island Parkway to Brooklyn.

Around an hour later, we were back in Floral Park, and I asked Tino where to drop him off as I couldn't wait to be rid of him. He said, "Take me to Big Daddy's house."

He asked me to go in with him, and I agreed, as I was curious to see Big Daddy again. We entered the somewhat worn-looking Cape house and headed down the hallway to the back bedroom. The door opened, and I saw three girls I recognized from the past summer hanging out in 172 Park sitting on a few beds. I was a bit shocked to see Big Daddy sitting there next to a glass with some liquid and several needles in it. He looked terrible, thin, and drawn, very different from the big strapping guy of a year earlier.

Tino looked at me and said, "Hey, you want to party with us?" I thought for a minute before agreeing. At that time, I was open to trying anything at least once.

I stuck out my arm so he could put the torniquet on, and he wrapped it around my forearm. Big Daddy asked if I had ever done this before, and I said no. One of the girls said, "I don't want to be here when he throws up," which made me a little nervous, as I didn't know what to expect.

I held out my arm and looked at Big Daddy. He looked up at me and said, "I'm not going to do this. I'm not going to be the one to give you your wings." He added, "This ain't like going out drinking with your friends."

They unwrapped the tourniquet and I left. Thankfully, I wound up never doing heroin, and I can only assume the worst would have happened in my life if he had made a different decision.

Talk about dodging a bullet! It was one of those fateful moments that made me think that maybe someone really was watching over me. When I told Phil about what happened, he was amazed, saying, "He never gave a f*ck about anyone his whole life."

Was someone watching over me? If they were, they may have saved my life.

I had the car for around six months, and, though it provided me with some fun and conveniences, I decided to sell it. I had wanted to drive and have my own car so badly, though the thought had occurred to me that instead of opening a new world, we might all just have our cars parked outside the handball courts and on Hillside Avenue. That pretty much became the case for most of us. We wound up standing around like we had been doing before we had cars.

But several months later, I felt it was the right time for another car. I found a 1966 Oldsmobile 442 that had a V8 engine, 4-barrel carburetor, and dual exhaust with extremely loud mufflers. I wasn't into a "fast" car, but this one was available and within my limited price range.

I was eighteen, had a car, and was relieved that high school was over. While working in Dan's Supermarket, I had the whole summer to think about what to do next, and I was generally optimistic.

Summer was moving along, and my disillusionment with the party scene was steadily increasing. More of us had cars, resulting in a shift from neighborhood hangouts like Hillside Avenue, Union Turnpike, and the schoolyard parks up to Alley Pond Park. The Big I had morphed into the "Turtle Guys," aptly named due to HT's old car that was bubble shaped and looked like a turtle shell. When that car would pull into the big parking lot on the upper level of Alley Pond Park off of Commonwealth Boulevard, someone yelled out something to the effect of "Hey, the Turtle Guys are here." The name stuck and lived on permanently.

I was heavily into the Grateful Dead, moving from loving their two studio albums into their live ones. I saw them live for the first time at Nassau Coliseum, and another band I started to like, New Riders of the Purple Sage, opened for them. It was one of my earliest concerts, and I really enjoyed it for the most part.

Hanging out in the park with my friends, listening to the Dead and the Allman Brothers was good fun, but something was missing. Looking around at everyone stoned out on various drugs or drunk and acting foolish, I began questioning if this was what I really wanted to be doing. One night, when I looked up at Creedmoor State Mental Hospital, which was nearby and visible, I wondered if the people hanging out in the park belonged in there instead of on the outside.

At the height of my disillusionment and toward the end of another night in the park, the song "Going Down the

Road Feeling Bad" covered by the Dead was blasting from some speakers on top of a car. I looked over and saw Tony Galioto, the guy I saw my first day of school outside JH 172. He had a knapsack, and I asked him what he was doing with that. He told me that he was going back to California . . . how he had been there and was going to hitch rides all the way back. I wished him good luck on his journey.

Tony made it back to LA and was shot to death in 1980 by police in a sting operation gone bad. I was given a copy of a newspaper article that described how Tony was a jerk, a two-bit dealer, but relatively harmless. They never found a weapon or drugs in the car he was in when this went down. Another sad story of a neighborhood guy whose life did not go well and ended early.

Having a car opened up some new opportunities with girls. Phil convinced me to go to a local club called Beau Brummel's to celebrate his eighteenth birthday. I reluctantly agreed, as that was not really my thing. I dressed the part with his help to pick out the right clothes.

While we were sitting at the bar, a group of girls came in, and I recognized one of them. She was very pretty and would say hello to me when we passed each other in the halls during school. She came right over to the bar and we started talking, so I bought her a drink and we went outside to make out. It was a one-time thing, but it was fun and great to be with such a pretty girl.

When we left the club, it was raining heavily, and we got into a car driven by a guy named Tommy. He was speeding down Hillside Avenue, made a sharp turn down a side street, and crashed into a fire hydrant. The engine looked to be severely damaged, with steam pouring out of the radiator. Phil looked at me and said, "Let's get out of here."

We proceeded to walk in the pouring rain at least half a mile to where his car was parked. We ended the night at a weird diner across the street from Creedmoor on Hillside Avenue. It was one fun and strange night that got me home at 4 a.m. When I arrived at work at 7 a.m., my boss looked at me and asked, "What happened to you?"

I told him I only had three hours of sleep. He responded, "That's more than I had." Typical of the times!

Shortly thereafter, I reconnected with Tina, the girl from Klein's, and we hung out and made it a few times. I would pick her up and we would listen to the Dead, make it, and go to a diner. Even though she was just a friend, which was totally fine with me, she would sleep with other guys.

One night, I went to pick her up, and some guy mockingly told me she was in the house screwing a guy who was a real piece of trash. He was ugly as sin and a degenerate, so I found it hard to believe. I was in my car listening to "Feeling Stronger Every Day" by Chicago when she came out of the house. We drove away, and when I asked her if it was true, she said yes.

That depressed me in a very deep way. I wondered how a girl who was such a nice and attractive person could wind up doing something like that. She obviously had issues, but this incident pushed me into a very dark place. I stopped seeing her after that and pretty much stopped socializing altogether. I would finish work at Dan's and just sit in my backyard listening to the Dead. I didn't want to hang out anymore. I wanted something different, but I didn't know what that was.

CHAPTER 11

The Cult

One of my coworkers at Dan's was kind of quiet and kept to himself, so I asked another guy what the story was with him. He told me, "Joe is some kind of Jehovah's Witness," which I had heard was some kind of religious group.

One day I asked Joe if that's what he was, and he said no. He then explained that he was a Christian and that his beliefs had changed his life. That piqued some level of interest on my part as it tied into the George Harrison music, the LSD experiences, and my spiritual curiosity. I had been approached by a Jehovah's Witness a brief time prior, gave it some thought, and never got into it.

One day, I was working out on the floor at Dan's, where the fruits and vegetables were displayed. Our job was to put up the displays, weigh the items, and mark the pricing on the bags for the customers. I noticed a girl come in, and she was getting some fruit weighed at the scale by Joe. They talked for a while, and I noticed that she was wearing a large wooden cross around her neck. I presumed she was Joe's girlfriend and didn't think much more about it.

I started to ask Joe more questions, and he gave me some basic materials that explained who Jesus was and some information on the four spiritual laws. He told me about a Bible study that he attended on Friday nights and asked me if I wanted to come and check it out. It was located somewhere in a town called East Meadow, which was around ten miles away in Nassau County. While it was a relatively short distance from our neighborhood, at that time, it may as well have been a different world from Queens. After giving it some thought, I decided to go and see what it was all about.

Joe picked me up for the ride out there, and when I got into his car, he said he had to pick up his girlfriend who lived in a town close by called New Hyde Park. I expected to see the girl who I noticed in the store with the wooden cross come out of the house. However, to my surprise, it was a different girl, and I wondered who that other girl from the store was.

We drove down Stewart Avenue through the affluent historical village of Garden City, which was a beautiful neighborhood lined by huge houses where several famous people have lived. Arriving in East Meadow after the short drive, I saw a nice, modern-looking church. Upon entering the lobby area, I saw several enclosed glass cases displaying various religious items. I took a seat in one of the chairs, and the place was buzzing with energy with many kids moving about who appeared to be around my age. Some of the pretty girls there would say hi to me as they walked by.

I noticed one of the girls looked familiar, and she walked by me a few times saying hi each time. She was the girl I had seen earlier, the one who I thought was Joe's girlfriend. She had short hair, having cut it since I first saw her, and she was really pretty. I later found out she was the younger sister of Joe's girlfriend.

Next, I entered a small conference room. Seated at the head of a table was a guy who was the teacher of the Bible study. I found the topic interesting, and the people in the room were very friendly.

After the study, we went downstairs to a full-size gymnasium with a basketball court. I joined in a light game with a few guys, which brought back some good memories. After the game, we all went to a local diner to hang out and talk. I liked the refreshing change from everything that had transpired and all the wildness of the past few years. I needed a change from hanging around in Alley Pond Park, and I thought maybe this would be it. I didn't realize at the time that, subconsciously, I was again searching for a family. This place and the people were starting to feel that way. I was being accepted for who I was, something I never experienced from my parents.

Joe was thrilled that I liked going there, and we kept talking at work. He told me that I had some admirers at the church, so I asked him what he was talking about. He said several of the girls there liked me, and I asked him which ones. He told me that Ann (his girlfriend Mary's sister) was one of them, which I really liked hearing, as I was very attracted to her.

Joe asked me if I wanted to go to another Friday night study the following week, and I agreed. He and Mary thought it would be good if I spoke to one of the other people there who they thought I could relate to. The purpose was to help me obtain a better understanding of what they were into. What they did not tell me was that I was being evangelized.

When we arrived, I noticed a short, heavy-set guy with blond hair and a full beard on the front lawn of the church. He was smoking a cigarette and had a Bible in his other hand. A pack of Marlboros protruded from the top pocket of his denim button-down shirt. He looked somewhat angelic, with a friendly face, big blue eyes, and a wide smile. He introduced himself as Ben.

We sat down on the grass, and he proceeded to tell me about the good things that the Lord had done in his life. How he himself was flawed, with problems like everyone has, yet found peace through his commitment to God. He was very likeable, as his hippie look and Marlboros gave him some level of credibility with me.

I thought about it all throughout the following week, and decided I would ask God into my life using the words provided in a pamphlet entitled "The Four Spiritual Laws." The last step was to go and tell someone you knew about the big step you had just taken. I promptly went to work at Dan's, and the acting manager, a guy they called "Niv," was assessing the inventory out on the floor. Niv was sort of a throwback to the pre-hippie times. He drank beer but wasn't a partier like the others at that time. He didn't do acid, and I never saw him even smoke a joint. He was what you might call old school. He seemed to get a kick out of how wild and different we "new schoolers" were. Eventually, as various groups within the neighborhood merged, Niv became a Turtle Guy.

As he was writing on his clipboard what items needed to be ordered, I said, "Niv, guess what?"

He looked at me with a devilish grin, awaiting my next words. I said, "I just accepted Jesus Christ as my personal Lord and Savior."

Shaking his head, he smiled and said, "You are completely burnt out of your freakin' mind."

That was the beginning of several encounters with the Turtle Guys, who were not happy about what my next steps would be.

I started going out with Joe, Mary, Ann, and others to movies and other group activities. When we went to see the movie *Paper Moon*, I told Ann I would pay for her. Standing a bit away from us, Joe quietly asked me if I minded paying for her, and I said in a drawn-out manner, "No." I found out later that Ann thought he had asked me if I liked her and that I had said no.

The various activities continued, and, a few weeks later before the Bible study, I asked Ann if she wanted to take a walk. She agreed, and as we strolled around the block, we kissed for the first time. It felt so good, and we held hands as we walked back to the church where Joe and Mary were both smiling from ear to ear when they saw us. They were hoping we would connect and were working behind the scenes to try and make that happen.

Ann looked younger than she was, and she was only sixteen-and-a-half at that time. I looked a little older than I was at eighteen, so it first appeared that she was perhaps too young for me. She had only one boyfriend before me, and even that was questionable due to the short duration and lack of interaction before she broke up with him.

What probably pushed her away from boys up to that point was that her father had left the family when she was thirteen. Divorce was heavily frowned upon at that time, especially within the Catholic Church. The bigger problem was that her father stopped all contact with the family. No phone calls, letters, or anything. It would be thirteen years before he suddenly reappeared, but the damage to the kids and Ann's mom was irreparable.

On our first official date, Mary and Ann cooked dinner for Joe and me. We had a genuinely nice time and then went to a small amusement park before ending the evening at Jones Beach, where Ann and I made out while sitting in the sand by the water.

While enjoying this new relationship and a religious awakening, things at home remained in a state of turmoil. One very bad incident took place between me and my father. I had borrowed the Grateful Dead album called *Live Dead* from a friend at work. It contained some intense music, and some believe it was the band at its best. "St. Stephen" was a hard-driving song that would evoke powerful feelings within me. I had a knack for electronics, and I had hooked up a basic stereo system in my room to an old Univox guitar amplifier to increase the volume.

One day I was playing the album at a very high volume, blasting that particular song. My father angrily yelled out to "Turn that shit off," which got me pretty mad.

Instead of turning it down, I turned the volume up. He came running up the stairs, and, after some words were exchanged, he proceeded to go to the stereo and punch down on the album while it was playing. I shouted at him, "It's not my album," along with some other choice words.

I always fought back verbally against him and my mother, but this time things got nasty, and we squared off. Even if I could have kicked his ass, which was highly unlikely, I did not have it in me to do something like that to my father. He, on the other hand, took it seriously and proceeded to punch me square in the nose, drawing blood. I have no idea how my nose did not break, as there was blood all over the place. I cursed him out as my mother yelled, "Look what you made him do." That was similar to a time when she was beating up my sister and yelling, "Look at her, she loves this, she's having an orgasm." My sister was sixteen when that happened, and I was seventeen at the time of that encounter with my father. I despised both of them and could not wait to get out of the house and live my own life. I knew I was a good person, but being there was bringing out the worst in me—and had been for several years.

Ann and I had been together a few months when Christmas rolled around. I bought her an ankle bracelet, which was the thing at the time to show others that you were a couple. She bought me a necklace that had a medal hanging from the chain with an impression of Jesus.

I truly appreciated the gift, though my father was pissed when he saw it and questioned why I would wear something like that. His attitude and what he said was hurtful to me and made me feel bad for Ann, who was thoughtful in choosing that gift for me.

It briefly diminished the joy I had derived from receiving it, but he didn't care. That was neither the first nor the last time he did something like that. There was never a thought or consideration of how his actions and words would hurt me.

I slept on the living room floor that Christmas Eve and could hear Ann's uncle sneak a few cigarettes from my pack while I was half-asleep. He was her mom's brother, and he lived with them in a very small apartment that had only one bedroom and a sort of big closet with bunk beds for her brother, Tom, and her uncle to sleep in. Her mom slept in the living room, and there was a small kitchen with a bathroom next to it. It was in New Hyde Park next to the Long Island Railroad tracks, so you would literally feel the vibration when a train would go by at the end of the block.

The only thing that separated the apartment from the tracks were a few warehouses. The family wound up there after their father had abandoned them while they were living in a nice house in Queens Village. Their mom held it together despite the terrible financial situation and trauma of what had happened. She took a few jobs waitressing at night so she could be home to help get the kids off to school.

A few weeks prior to meeting Ann, I was driving with John toward Hempstead to pick up some parts for my car. Driving down Jericho Turnpike in New Hyde Park, I noticed a small diner, and I asked John if he wanted to grab something to eat. The waitress was extremely friendly, and I even mentioned it to John on the way out.

Ann, her sister, and her mom were very warm, loving people. I connected with them immediately as they were so different from my parents. The love and acceptance I had been denied had me searching for that. Whether it was Phil's family, the Turtle Guys, or the good people from other families, it was what I desperately needed. They were all a type of surrogate family. This has been described by experts as one of the keys to recovering from child abuse and trauma.

One of the first nights after Ann and I got together, she and I, Joe, Mary, and Tom were all hanging out on the steps outside her apartment. It was late, and we ran out of cigarettes. Tom said there was a cigarette machine up on Jericho Turnpike. When we pulled up to the diner, I mentioned that I had just been there recently. I also told them that there was a really nice waitress there, and Tom asked me if she was short and chubby. I said yes, and he said, "That was my mother." I thought he was joking, but he wasn't. I had actually met my mother-in-law before I met my wife. Strange, small-world occurrence!

Steadily moving into my new world was not without its complications. One of the conditions required to be considered a believer was to not get high anymore. This meant no more weed or anything else. I was also required to leave my old friends behind, as they would likely be a bad influence. Both those things had been my so-called saving grace in dissociating myself from the trauma and abuse at home, so I had to make some tough decisions. I had a setback, and, when I explained this to Ann and Joe, they suggested I speak to someone at the church. I made an appointment with a pastor there to try and get some guidance regarding the transitional challenges I was facing.

When we did meet, he was very understanding and compassionate. At the end of our conversation, he asked me if I would pray with him, and I agreed. I really felt something as we were praying, and, right afterward, I felt something like a positive, uplifting glow from within. I was ready to move ahead, though it would require the steps of commitment.

I had to break from the friends with whom I shared a special bond. They had accepted me when I was lost and dealing with all sorts of difficulties. When Johnny realized what was happening, he became terribly upset. One day in the back room at Dan's, he just looked at me and cried.

"What are you doing?" he asked me.

I couldn't answer, but it really upset me. Niv was so upset, he called me a "Jesus freak" and wanted me to meet his cousin (who was a priest) to talk some sense into me. Phil was somewhat understanding, but he himself did not want any part of it.

One Saturday night, I was alone, as Ann was invited to a wedding. She was also in the bridal party, while I wasn't invited. I had nothing to do and wound up driving up to Alley Pond Park where the guys were hanging out. I got into their car, and they were all smoking pot. When I declined to partake, they started asking me why. One guy asked if I thought they were all going to hell. It was not a pleasant experience.

New Year's Eve had me questioning what I was doing. The initial honeymoon phase of the Bible studies had worn off, and I realized I was not like many of the people involved there. There were some real nerds, different from both me and the people where I came from. One of them threw a New Year's Eve party at his house. I decided to go, as this is what those people did.

Around midnight, I told John that there was a Grateful Dead concert being broadcast live on the radio. We went into the living room and turned it on. The guy whose house it was (his name was Artie) also came into the room. When he realized what we were listening to, he shut it off and said, "We only listen to Christian music in this house."

That really ticked me off. I was starting to feel like that was not the place for me. Although there were a few exceptions, the people there were not cut from the same cloth that I was.

Several years later, a few friends and I were talking about Artie and how strange he was. A mutual friend commented that Artie was a rare individual who actually achieved all of his fantasies. He had been in a biker gang, played in a rock band, joined the Israeli army, became a rabbi, and wound up interviewed in a documentary on TV about the end times.

Later that night, we went to the house of a guy named Robby. We sat in his basement doing basically nothing, and I was bored to tears. Drinking was frowned upon and several people, myself included, had vowed to give up cigarettes starting at midnight. I began to think about another party I had been invited to at a guy's house back in the neighborhood. I struggled internally, as part of me wanted to go and see all my old friends to celebrate like we had the previous few years. But I knew that if I went there, I would probably wind up back in a world that the other part of me no longer wanted any part of.

I finally got fed up and said to John, "Let's get out of here."

So we walked out and opened the doors to his '65 GTO. Inside was a bag of Ann's clothing, as the plan was that she would sleep over with a group of girls at one of their houses. I took the bag out of the car and placed it on top of another car.

As John made the U-turn to leave, Ann came running out of the house crying. She asked where I was going, so

I told her. If we had left a minute earlier, it probably would have resulted in the end of our relationship, as I knew that returning to my old friends that night would have, in all likelihood, ended my religious adventure.

A group gathered to find out what was going on and what the problem was. Ben had a calming effect on me, so I told him that I wanted to leave and why. After I calmed down, Ben suggested that John, Joe, and I sleep over at his house to take a breath, to just talk and reevaluate things.

"How are we going to do that if we don't have any cigarettes?" I asked.

"I have a whole carton at my house," Ben replied.

We all laughed and were relieved knowing that the carton would help us get through the night and any heavy discussions.

It was another example of a situation in which life could have gone either way. If we had left a minute earlier after John turned his car around, my life may have turned out very differently. Was it really fate or just random luck?

Ann and I married two years later. I was twenty and she was eighteen-and-a-half. We were so young, yet we were determined to be together. We had both experienced different traumas in our childhood, and the idea of being on our own and starting a new life together was very appealing.

We had no money, but it was still very exciting to get our first apartment, which her mom helped us find. It was in the general area of the neighborhood of New Hyde Park, the second floor of a meticulously kept house owned by a landscaper. The outside of the house was a sort of show-case with rocks and little waterfalls, beautiful shrubbery, and a manicured lawn.

Due to our lack of money, we had to wait for the wedding gifts (cash) to buy a refrigerator. I would put the milk outside of a window in our kitchen on the roof of a garage to keep it cold and fresh. We initially had only a few pieces of furniture and slept in a single bed until the father of a friend of Ann's donated a twin bed to us. Despite it all, we were happy to be independent and in our own place together.

Although the general custom is that the family of the bride pays for the wedding, Ann's mom did not have the means to do that. I was pleasantly surprised that my parents volunteered to cover it, but then, of course, they wanted complete control of everything. I was advised to choose my battles carefully in that situation and fight only for what was really important. I followed that advice, and when it came to friends I could invite and the ceremony, we stuck to what we wanted. My mother started playing her games when it came to her family. She invited her sister's family, including children, and one of her brother's family, excluding the children.

That led to my grandfather and father getting into a big argument, the result of which was that my grandfather told him, "None of us are coming."

My entire family from back in Brooklyn, my root from birth into the initial stages of my life, would not be there on one of the most important days of my life. It was a battle I chose not to fight with everything else going on, but it hit home on my joyous wedding day. I was very sad that my family was not there to celebrate with me.

My parents' behavior remained consistent, though my mother would almost always take the lead. Every joyous occasion was marred by some ridiculous thing she would conjure up to cause problems. We were told that none of us would attend my sister's wedding, which is something I regret going along with to this day. My brother had his clothes thrown out of the house onto the front lawn because my mother did not like the place he and his fiancée had chosen to have their wedding. My mother also fired up my father against his boss, who was a part owner of the company. One of her tactics was to have my father invite all the other management and exclude his boss. That strategy worked well when, shortly thereafter, my father was fired from a job he loved. It didn't take a genius to figure out that if you continuously irritate your boss, who is an owner, you might wind up out the door.

Things at the church went well in those early days. The activities were wholesome, and I was enjoying learning many new things from the sermons and Bible studies. I was even asked to fill in one Sunday morning to teach a children's Bible study. I had never done anything like that before, and, though I was a bit nervous, I enjoyed it and got through it okay. Public speaking was something I dreaded back then, though on the ride home I felt a profound sense of accomplishment.

I attended a retreat in upstate New York where the church had rented a facility containing cabins with sleeping areas and a main room for meetings. I drove up at night with a couple of the guys, and the first night we just crashed in our bunk beds in one of the rooms of a cabin.

The next morning, we all met in a large room where we were served breakfast, and a study on the book of Timothy ensued, with one of the pastors leading it. After the study, we were told to walk around the grounds and think about what we had just learned. It was early winter, and outside it was extremely quiet and peaceful. The icicles dangling from the trees gave the appearance of a winter wonderland.

As I walked alone with my new Bible in hand, I was enjoying nature and a sense of spiritual connection to my Creator. Those early days were good, and I was happy in my new life and what felt like family, away from the turbulence of my teen years.

Back home, following the retreat, I felt renewed and started to attend Sunday night services that were given at another church in a nearby town. Ben had asked me if I ever heard the preacher there, and when I told him I hadn't, he said, "You're really in for a treat."

It was a packed house, and the preacher there was dynamic. I hung on to every word and was somewhat surprised at my ability to really comprehend the messages within the sermon. I had never heard anything like that before and found it fascinating.

At the end of the service, a few members who were Jewish were called up to the altar. A prayer shawl, called a "tallit" in Hebrew, would be wrapped around them as a prayer for Israel was offered up. Those members were referred to as "Hebrew Christians," and I found that to be comforting, unique, and interesting.

Over time, the teaching began to focus increasingly on Israel and how Jesus and his followers were practicing Jews. This gave me a level of comfort, especially because I often felt like an outcast during my teen years. Being the only Jew among twenty plus Irish and Italian friends was a little strange, as that was not the norm. Even though I was fully accepted, it felt awkward at times, especially when I would occasionally hear an anti-Semitic remark.

Not all members of the church were on board with the advent of practicing Jewish customs, while others fully embraced it. An additional Saturday night service was added that included Hebrew prayers. Holidays were especially enjoyable, as singing and dancing to Jewish spiritual folk songs were part of the celebrations. It was a time of great learning for me. My early years of IGC designation and being an SP student gave me the confidence to help learn all the new things. I dug in and started to become more respected by other members as my knowledge began to grow.

What started out as born-again Christianity gradually became Hebrew Christianity and then morphed into a strange form of Judaism. Several members were starting to practice Jewish laws and customs, and I was constantly reading books written by Christian scholars with titles like

The Crucifixion of the Jews, Jesus and the Zealots, and many others. A form of Jewish mysticism called Kabbalah also captured my attention, and I bought a set of books called *The Zohar* which contained mystical writings that I found very interesting.

Education and career advancement were both encouraged, and many people were going to school to start a degree program or returning to obtain advanced degrees. Others were starting new careers or opening businesses.

That encouragement had a major impact on me personally. I started college right after high school. In choosing to get married so young, however, I had to work and earn a living. This limited me to school at night. I bounced around some jobs to make money while Ann was also working in New York City as a secretary. We barely made ends meet, and I could not seem to find the right fit. I wanted and needed an opportunity, something I could put myself into wholeheartedly. I wanted to learn and grow in whatever that would be, and I prayed for it.

Many of my Turtle Guy friends had gone into blue collar jobs. Civil service, sanitation, police work, firefighting, and other unionized jobs were where most of those folks wound up. I thought about doing that and tried one job in the post office but realized it was not for me.

The friends I had from earlier years who were highly focused on education mostly went directly to college and wound up in either medicine, law, or business. I realized that was the direction I wanted to go and decided to go back to school full time and work part time.

So, in the winter of 1978, I started at Nassau Community College. I felt so awkward and embarrassed the first few days there, as most of the students were a few years younger than me. I soon recognized one of the guys from the church who was around my age, and we started hanging around together at school. We were pretty close in the grades we achieved; he had a 4.0 and I had a 3.6 GPA. We both made the dean's list, and I realized that I was still somewhat smart, which gave me motivation and confidence to keep going.

The other guy was single and able to go to school full time and also hold a full-time job. Being married and having financial pressures, I could not do the same thing.

After completing his two years at Nassau, my friend won a scholarship to NYU and ultimately became a successful CEO of a company. For me, it would be a longer road to success. But I kept at it, taking classes at night and on weekends while working.

Buddhism teaches that what seems like the worst thing in life is actually the best thing. One of the jobs I had while going to school let me go. I was railroaded by a girl who worked behind the scenes to get me fired. The other guys who worked there saw it and expressed their sympathy to me while confirming that I got a raw deal. At that time, Ann and I were living in a basement apartment in Elmont, and, while she went to work, I tried to find another job while spending my days in the lousy apartment, somewhat depressed from being unemployed.

One of the guys from the church was having a party, and my wife encouraged me to go. I was down and didn't want to, though I finally gave in. Once there, I struck up a conversation with Andy and asked what he was doing. He told me he had recently started working for a freight forwarder at JFK airport. I asked him how he got the job, and it was through his sister's connection. He then told me they were hiring and asked if I was interested. I said, "Yes, definitely."

Getting that job kicked off a career which would take me on a journey through international banking and, ultimately, into related information technology. I would wind up traveling to twenty-two countries around the world, becoming a vice president of a bank, and a director at one of the largest IT companies in the world. Worst thing, best thing?

Ann and I found a better apartment at the time our first child was born, a lovely baby girl named Eleanor. I continued in freight forwarding and it was good; however, Andy and I were always strategizing about our careers. He was a very smart guy who early on had considered going to medical school, but circumstances and his independent streak took him into the business world instead. We mutually decided that working in a bank would be better for both our careers and our finances. At that time, banks had great tuition reimbursement benefits that I knew could really help me accelerate my goal of obtaining a bachelor's degree.

There was a banking component within the freight forwarding business, and, ultimately, the experience we derived gave us the skills that banks were looking for.

I obtained my first banking job and commuted to New York City where the bank was located, on Broadway near the World Trade Center and Wall Street. A few years earlier, one of my jobs had me assisting a guy who had a route in downtown Manhattan. Sitting in his truck, I would see all these people relaxing outside the office buildings at lunchtime and wonder how someone would get there. Through hard work, perseverance, and inner drive, I became one of those people.

Everything was moving in a good direction, but things at the church (or now, "community," as it was being called) were changing. The time of innocence and freedom had changed to a more structured regimen.

Rules and restrictions were implemented by the leadership, which was composed of twelve Elders who were responsible for governing the community. They sat under the main leader, one of the pastors who was highly intelligent and charismatic, with impressive oratory skills.

He established what was called a "Covenant Community," a subset of the larger church, open by invitation to those who just enjoyed worshipping and the fellowship that was offered. To be a member of the Covenant Community, one had to be a born Jew or be "adopted" into the leader's family. I had my doubts and met with the leader to discuss them, and, after I explained, he told me, "You're not committed."

I disputed that as strictly adhering to the rules; leaving my friends and my former lifestyle were, in my mind, acts of a deep commitment. However, I was told that where this was heading would require a deeper level of commitment. I decided to join, and, looking back, it was probably something I needed to prove to myself that I was ready and could do it.

The Elders were appointed at an initial community dinner that the leader had arranged. After a dinner where the main dish was lamb, the group of maybe a hundred people were asked to nominate those they thought should be an Elder. Once someone was nominated, people were allowed to express their opinion as to whether they agreed with the nomination. One after the other, people would step up to the microphones set up at the four corners of the room to offer up their thoughts regarding the nominee being discussed. I was shocked when an older gentleman who was highly respected nominated me.

I was relatively new to everything there, while others had been part of the overall group for many years. I didn't realize it at the time, but being judged like that brought back subconscious thoughts of my mother berating me as a child.

I was nervous as one person after another stood up to offer opinions about me and my ability to fill the job. When I was asked how I felt about it, I stood up and said I believed I could do the job well and expressed some reasons why. After all the opinions had been expressed, the leader would close his eyes and announce the decision. In my case, he said, "Rory, you will not be an Elder."

My heart sank, and I felt embarrassed and hurt. I then had to face all these people feeling like I was a failure. It hit on all my insecurities from the abuse, and the feeling was similar to when I read the names of finalists who made the junior high basketball team and my name wasn't there. I felt like running out of the room and never going back.

When the meeting broke up, one of the pastors came over to me and said, "This will now be your real test."

I thought about that on the ride home, and those words helped me to continue. I wish someone, perhaps one of my parents, had had the wisdom to teach me that when I encountered failures while growing up. That event taught me a great lesson, which is to pick yourself up when you get knocked down. It's called grit, and many experts have written how that characteristic is the number one determinant for success in life.

I persevered with more determination than ever to learn and grow spiritually. People seemed to have a greater respect for me just for getting nominated. As the community was delving deeper into Jewish practices, I studied hard to learn as much as I could, and my knowledge of Jewish law, history, language, and customs continued to grow.

I even attended a Shabbat with the Hasidic Jewish sect called the Lubavitcher in Crown Heights, Brooklyn. I had encountered them when they were investigating our group because they were interested as to why a group of mostly Christians were practicing Judaism. They invited me and a friend as a way to show us what real Judaism was. They wanted to "rescue" born Jews if they could.

It was before sundown on Friday evening when they brought us to their main synagogue and world headquarters, located at 770 Eastern Parkway. There a group assembled in a small room for preliminary prayers. In walked the famous Rebbe Menachem Schneerson, the leader of the sect who was revered by many in the Orthodox community. They placed us very close to him during prayer, believing that would somehow have a positive effect on moving us toward their beliefs. After prayer at the synagogue, they split us up, and we each stayed overnight with different families for the traditional Sabbath meal.

All day Saturday was spent in the synagogue praying and listening to the Rebbe's teachings, which were translated from Yiddish into English for our benefit. At one point, the Rebbe would look over the large assembly, and if you stood up and raised your small cup of wine, he might nod, an acknowledgement of his blessing. I stood up, sticking out like a sore thumb with my long hair and maroon-colored suit, and the Rebbe gave me his blessing. It was an overall positive experience as I somehow felt a connection with it all, knowing that this was what my ancestors had been doing for centuries prior to arriving in America.

The weekend ended with an interesting occurrence. When my friend and I had arrived on Friday, we were unable to find the address on President Street. One of the Hasidic men, seeing that we looked confused, asked if he could help. He then walked us to our destination.

Ironically, as we were leaving after Shabbat on Saturday night and were heading to where our car was parked, the last person we saw was the same guy. He waved to us and we waved back. We had not encountered him the entire time we were there, and it seemed a bit strange that the guy who helped us enter was the same guy who saw us upon our exit. It felt like a bookend.

Back in our world, people started coming to me for help in understanding certain practices within Judaism. Most of the community members were from Christian backgrounds, primarily Lutheran. Jews were a minority.

The following year, it was time to either keep, remove, or replace the Elders. As Ann and I were entering the church, I told her how relieved I was that I would not have to go through what I went through the year before. Yet, incredibly, the same gentleman who nominated me the year prior nominated me again. I couldn't believe it, and I was concerned that I would get rejected again. However, one person after another got up and said very positive things about me and their belief that I should be selected. The big moment came, and I heard the words: "Rory, you will be an Elder."

I was relieved, as it felt like getting the job you really wanted. Despite my battle with the insecurities resulting from childhood trauma, I had a deep belief in myself. I think it came primarily from the love and nurturing that I received from my grandmother during those formative years when I was with her all the time.

The enthusiasm that accompanied becoming part of the leadership at the age of twenty-one was short-lived, as, soon thereafter, things began to unravel. Out of nowhere, we were told by the leader that Ann and I would need to make a deeper commitment.

Our mission was to prepare for the end times by learning and participating in survivalist training. Training would include camping, hiking, learning map and compass techniques, canoeing, bow and arrow skills, and self-sufficiency farming, all of which was geared to surviving the calamities of the tribulation and end times.

The new direction was a major departure from the initial goals of the community and raised serious questions for Ann and me. Previously, the main focus was on the practice of Jewish laws and customs as a means of identification with Jesus and his Jewish followers.

Our doubts continued to grow, when, at the end of a Shabbat service, the leader announced he was disbanding the community. He proclaimed that we were free to leave if we wanted to and there would be no repercussions. His cryptic announcement left everyone wondering what was going on, and rumors began to fly. People were hurt, confused, and struggling to try and make sense of it all.

During this time of turmoil, other disturbing things were exposed concerning the alleged behavior and practices some of the leaders had been involved in. Allegations were made regarding pedophilia and other abuses, shaking members to the core.

Upon hearing about the pedophilia and the extremely disturbing explanations and justifications, Ann immediately decided to leave the cult. Debate and soul-searching continued among the members, and many decided to leave while others needed more convincing or remained committed. Brainwashing runs deep within cults, making those decisions quite difficult. It is agonizing for people to realize that years of their lives were spent deeply believing in something that turned out to be a fraud.

It was an excruciatingly difficult decision to make, and, initially, I had very mixed emotions. On the one hand, I felt free for the first time in years, while, on the other hand, my belief system was shattered. I remember looking at all the books on my bookcase covering various aspects of Judaism, Christianity, and Islam. I treasured those wonderful books that I had read or studied from. As I stared at them, I felt sad, knowing how serious and devoted I had been. Yet I found myself wondering if it was all a waste of time: if it was nothing more than bullshit.

I spent nine years of my early adult life involved in this religious community before things unraveled. People who are in a cult like we were don't realize what they are really involved with. Lies are mixed with truths, and, in many cases, the leaders are very smart and manipulative. People from all different backgrounds were members. Doctors, lawyers, politicians, bankers, police, and teachers were all involved. An investigator who had worked on bringing members of the Hare Krishnas to justice was asked how people who had started out with peaceful intentions wound up committing many heinous crimes. He replied, "The need for something to believe in for absolutes . . ."[4]

One day, shortly after leaving the cult, I was in my parents' house in a downstairs room where there were a bunch of old record albums. I had been away from music that I loved for many years, as rock music was frowned upon for not being spiritually edifying. I threw on a Beatles album, and the first song I heard after all that time was "Strawberry Fields." I felt chills hearing the opening melody. After listening to the song, it hit me how I had been living in a very narrow-minded way for a long time. It felt like I had come home after a long, strange journey, wondering where I had been all those years.

The challenge that followed for us was the need to reconstruct our lives and belief systems. Many ex-members of the cult were struggling with what they would do next regarding religion and spirituality. One friend jokingly said he did not know what to do now on Saturdays: go fishing or to a synagogue for Sabbath services. Though his comment was somewhat amusing, it captured the confusion people were experiencing after leaving. What we wholeheartedly believed in, sacrificed for, and were deeply committed to was suddenly gone. Left behind were many questions, pain, and confusion.

Ann and I decided we would take our time and not rush into anything new. We needed some guidance to help us and thought it would be a good idea to consult with some rabbis. We started by going back to my old neighborhood, which could at times be a source of comfort when things in life got tough.

The first rabbi we met with was from the Hebrew school I went to as a child. He was suspicious and arrogant and condescending to us. The second was from the Orthodox Temple, and he was adamant regarding certain laws that would apply to my wife as a convert. Those initial meetings were not helpful and just further alienated us.

The next rabbi, who I'll refer to as Rabbi Ari, was a kind and brilliant man who was also a great teacher. I had met him a few years earlier at a rally outside Yankee Stadium where we joined a large gathering of people there to hear Reverend Sun Myung Moon speak. Moon was a Korean leader of The Unification Church who claimed to be a messiah. The reason we were there was to try and meet others we believed were being deceived and going down the wrong path.

At the time I did not realize that I was one of those people, just in a different cult. The rabbi who was there for the same reasons I was had been moving through the crowd when he saw that we were doing something similar. He came up to John (who was also with me at the time) and me to ask if I was Jewish. When I told him I was, he asked me to call him and we exchanged phone numbers.

A brief time later, I went with another friend to Rabbi Ari's temple in the Riverdale section of the Bronx for a class he was teaching. He was a very dynamic and impressive speaker. He spoke about the time when he asked his father, who was a Holocaust survivor, what he was thinking about when he was in a concentration camp. His father referred to the passage from the book of Ezekiel in which God would bring dry bones back to life (Ezek. 37:1–10). He said that is what he thought about; it was also what kept him going.

When the cult blew up, I met with the rabbi and explained what had happened. He then also agreed to meet other ex-members, regardless of their religious backgrounds, to provide counseling or guidance. He extended himself by offering that help without prejudgment. That was exactly what the ex-members needed, and they deeply appreciated his efforts.

During our discussions, I asked him what would happen to me when I died if I decided not to be observant. I told him how I believed that the religion most people take on is very often a product of where they were raised and their family beliefs. How it would be just as difficult for a religious person to adapt to my earlier nonreligious life, as it would be for me to adapt to theirs.

He told me that if I ever again decided to do anything religiously, it would need to well up from within myself and not from any outside influences. He said that the important thing was not if or how observant I would ever be; it was to continue questioning and remain in the struggle. His compassion and understanding were greatly appreciated and helped me move ahead without a cloud of guilt.

We were living in Elmont, New York, at that time, so we decided to check out the local synagogue. There, we met with another rabbi who happened to have gone to school with Rabbi Ari from Riverdale. He was also a very understanding and compassionate man who had a PhD in psychology and was teaching at Hofstra University.

Ann was considering conversion, so we agreed to meet with him for her to have one-on-one classes working toward that goal. The three of us would meet first before her class, and then I would leave and pick her up when they finished.

One time I asked him how he interpreted the verse from the book of Malachi 4:5 that states, "Behold, I will send you Elijah the prophet before the great and terrible day of the Lord." He responded, saying, "That's a nice idea."

I was shocked that he did not interpret that verse literally. When I asked, he explained that throughout religious history, there were references to a golden era of the past and a golden era of the future. How that gave people hope in their often-dire circumstances. Initially, I was blown away by this, though, when I really thought about what he said, it made sense.

In Christianity, there was both the time Jesus was on earth and his anticipated return in the future. In Judaism, there was the Kingdom of David in the past and when the Messiah will come in the future. When I left the meeting on that crisp fall night, I lit a cigarette, looked up at the sky, and thought to myself, *I think that somehow the rabbi just convinced me not to believe in God!*

It was a while later when I realized that what he had done was actually brilliant. He knew that we were coming from a fundamentalist mentality. In order to break that, it would be better to smash that mentality and have us go from there. The combination of him doing that and what Rabbi Ari had counseled led us to the decision the healthiest thing for us to do would be to take a break from all of it.

We started to live like the people we really were, though initially it wasn't easy. On our first visit to Burger King, I almost gagged knowing I was eating non-Kosher meat.

One of the first things I did after our decision to leave the cult was to call my old buddy Phil. We had not been in contact for several years, and I think he was shocked to hear from me, but he was very happy. Since our days working in the post office after high school, we had gone in totally different directions. He joined the NYPD after the seven or so years he remained in the post office job.

I told him of my decision and asked if he wanted to get together to talk. When he agreed, I asked when, thinking maybe in a few weeks. He asked me, "How about tomorrow?"

I happily agreed, and, the next night, there we were like old times, with him at the wheel. This time, we were on the Cross Island Parkway heading toward Brooklyn to a bar he liked. He asked me to tell him more of the details of what happened, and, in the process of doing that, I expressed some guilt about my decision.

People can be affected for the rest of their lives after leaving a cult. In my search for a surrogate family, the cult provided many of the things I yearned for: living what I thought was the right way, camaraderie, fellowship, participating in wholesome activities, helping each other, focusing on education, trying to do the right things, and love that was initially unconditional. There were good things mixed in that gave me a sense of what a family should be.

In his inimitable way, Phil made some amusing comments to help me realize that I had made the right decision. At one point he shouted, "What do you want me to do, deprogram you? Yell shit at you? I'll do that if you want me to."

It was funny, and it did help me. It was great to have our friendship, which was really a brotherly relationship, renewed.

The other person who helped me greatly at that time was my brother-in-law Tommy, who was more like a brother to me. He and my sweet mother-in-law were greatly relieved by our exit from the cult. Although Tom was in the heyday of his "hanging out" phase, partying and being with girls (whom he attracted like a magnet), he wanted to spend time with me. I told him he didn't have to do that, that I knew he had better things to do on Friday nights.

He insisted, so we would meet up and drive around and wind up at a diner or local bar. I explained to him that I wasn't sure what to do or how to be anymore.

Tom was always joking, an all-around "class clown" kind of guy who would keep up a tough exterior. Yet underneath it all was a very smart, sensitive, and caring person. He provided me with some insightful and important words of wisdom, saying, "You will probably try several different things and in the long run wind up being who you really are."

That is ultimately what happened. We became even closer after that and would spend a good deal of time together from then on.

My mother-in-law, Franny, was a very kind and good-hearted soul, and those great attributes were passed down to her three children: Tom, Mary, and my wife, Ann. Though the family was left in dire financial straits after being deserted by Franny's husband, she did everything possible to provide for her children and give them a good upbringing. She was a loving and nurturing soul who gave of herself to others despite her own difficulties, and many gravitated to her for advice and companionship.

I remember one night that really touched me was when she babysat my older daughter Eleanor while Ann and I were meeting with the rabbi in Elmont. It was a freezing, wintry night and there were piles of snow and ice all around.

After our meeting, I drove her home and offered to walk her up to her apartment inside the court of the complex she lived in, but she declined. As I saw her making her way around the snow and ice, it broke my heart how, after a day of work, she would sacrifice due to her enduring love for us, especially her first grandchild. After a lengthy battle with cancer, she passed away in 1989 and is greatly missed by all who knew her.

Andy and I went to work for another freight forwarder and spent a brief time there learning more about the banking side of exporting and importing. Andy had helped me get the job with the small family-owned company, and, when I started, they were located in the World Trade Center (WTC) on the 80th floor of one of the towers. After a brief time, they relocated to 90 West Street, which was right across from the garage where the first WTC bombing took place in 1993.

After gaining that experience, we strategized and agreed that a move into the banks would benefit our careers. We both wound up getting jobs in different banks that were also located in downtown Manhattan. I joined Marine Midland Bank at 140 Broadway while Andy went to Chase, located on Water Street.

Working at Marine had its good and bad points. It allowed me to start a new career in trade finance, building upon the experience I had obtained. The bank would also pay for me to continue my education toward a bachelor's degree, which I knew would be necessary for my career advancement. They paid 100 percent in advance for all courses related to a business degree.

The downside was that the place was a zoo. Bank operations was a rough area to work in, especially trade finance. The pressures were great because an incorrect decision could cause the bank to lose significant amounts of money. The people who worked there could be rough-edged, as these were not the "elite" management trainees who would wind up in the quiet offices with plush carpeting, smoking pipes. That is where the graduates from Harvard and Wharton worked. Operations was loud, and there were often periods of infighting and screaming, as personality conflicts were common. I did not know what I would be walking into when I started there, but, from experience, I knew how to adapt and deal with difficult situations in order to survive.

A huge positive of the job was that due to the nature of the work being international trade and banking, the staff was composed of people from several different nationalities and races. In my department there were Indians, Pakistanis, Arabs, Chinese, Iranians, Filipinos, and others. The Americans were Black, White, and Latino.

Most of my friends and family members did not get to experience the type of interactions I had with people from all those diverse cultures. Since childhood, I had had a curiosity about other neighborhoods and cultures, so I found that part of the job quite interesting and educational. As a result of my interactions, I even wound up learning some basic Urdu, the language spoken in Pakistan.

I was truly driven and kept learning and absorbing all I could. I knew that I had been given a terrific opportunity, and I was going to seize it. The head of our department was a vice president considered to be a guru of the business. When anyone had a difficult problem, he was the guy to go to help resolve it. He was also teaching classes at the American Bankers Association, which really impressed me. I was told that he had previously worked for the sanitation department and had worked his way up within the bank. I was inspired and, after some thought, I established similar career goals. I wanted to become both a VP and a teacher within my field.

After two years at Marine Midland Bank, Andy asked me to join him at Chase, and I decided to do it. The year I spent there helped me expand my knowledge and experience, and it was another key step toward achieving my goals.

One morning, as I was walking to my desk, a colleague from India who I had never spoken to asked me if I wanted a new job. That question and my response would lead to another strange adventure.

By that time, we had had outgrown our one-bedroom apartment and moved into a larger one. We were fortunate to get this place. Phil's dad, who was like a father to me, had a connection at a local garden apartment complex. Phil had just moved in there, and I thought it would be great to live so close to each other as adults like when we did when we were kids. The rent on the new apartment was significantly higher than the one we were in, but we did not have many choices in that tight housing market. I finalized the details with Phil's dad and thanked him for helping me out.

"You are damn near like a son to me," he said.

I was deeply moved by his words, as help like that wasn't something I was used to. Help from my own parents was rare—even when I seriously needed it—though after some coaxing, my father did agree to cosign the lease agreement on the apartment.

My wife was pregnant, due soon, and would not be going back to work in the foreseeable future. Money was tight, and the idea of a higher salary was very appealing. I asked Ashish if the bank was a foreign bank and if they were located in Midtown. He said yes to both questions, which sounded perfect and exactly what I was looking for. The anticipated extra money was a great incentive to explore making the move. He jotted down the contact's name, phone number, and the name of the bank. It was one I had never heard of: BCCI.

BCCI (Bank of Credit and Commerce International) was located at 375 Park Avenue, which was a prime New York City location. I mentioned to a colleague and friend of mine who was Pakistani that I had an interview with that bank.

"Oh that's great," he said. "If they like you and you get hired, you will be set for life."

I was surprised and asked him what he meant. I was highly skeptical of anything this guy would say, as he was a bit of a wild card. He told me that the bank was loaded from laundering drug money and that was the reason they had decided to open a bank. I laughed him off, thinking the guy was really crazy.

I sat down in a conference room in a very nice office for my first interview. It went well, and the manager who interviewed me told me that their culture and the way they did banking was quite different from the way Chase and other US banks did it. I told him I could adapt and did not think much more about it.

A week or so later, I was asked to come in for a second interview and mentioned it to my Pakistani friend. He happened to know the personnel manager at the bank and told me the interview would be very important for me. Then I would be interviewed by the general manager (GM) of the branch and a decision would be made.

It was the strangest interview I ever had. The GM was impeccably dressed in an expensive suit and walked around seemingly disorganized while puffing on a cigar. I sat in front of his desk and three other guys who also sat facing him: the personnel manager, the guy who initially interviewed me, and another manager.

I was ready to answer questions and sell myself as one would do in a typical interview. He would pick up a note from his desk and walk away. He asked me one or two business questions, and then he asked if I was married. I told him I was and that my wife was pregnant. Then he stood up, as did the other guys, so I followed.

He reached out to shake my hand and said, "May God give you a son."

I did not know what that meant, as the other guys were all smiling. They all shook my hand and congratulated me, confirming I got the job!

My wife gave birth to a beautiful baby girl two weeks before my starting date. I now had two baby girls and was a proud father. From my experience in the cult and in studying other religions, I found it deeply upsetting and despicable how the more fanatical aspects of religion look down upon women. To them it was some sort of curse for girls to be born instead of boys. For me it was another item added to my list of things I found confusing and distasteful about organized religion.

I started my new job at a time when I was plagued by other conflicts in addition to religious ones. Though I did not realize it at the time, they stemmed from the childhood trauma I had endured. I felt as if I had failed and that no matter what I tried to do to succeed in my career financially, I came up short. I felt like the Jewish people I grew up with were all successful and living wonderful lives. The non-Jews were all doing well in their secure civil service and other blue collar, mostly unionized jobs, and here I was, unfulfilled in my job working for people from a different country and culture. I felt somewhat trapped, being married with two young children and struggling financially with no real light at the end of a long tunnel.

Seeing the glass half empty was what I always heard and saw from my parents while growing up. They were always comparing themselves to others trying to, as said in the idiom, "keep up with Jones's." I thought it was absurd when I observed and heard those things from them, but that mentality had worked its way into my thinking. Their outlook toward life combined with the never-ending verbally abusive comments directed at everyone had a terrible effect on me. My mother was miserable, an admittedly unhappy person who could never appreciate the things she did have, which is truly sad.

I learned later on that childhood trauma can—and often will—trigger memories of the trauma even years later. I also came to understand how those triggers are subconscious: some refer to them as tapes that play in the mind. When you don't know where these memories are coming from, you don't have much of a defense, and those thoughts can be extremely debilitating and destructive. Low self-esteem and depression are typical results, which can lead to various self-destructive behaviors.

I had been battling these things for many years, though in the cult as a leader at the age of twenty-one, they became more obvious. I was under pressure to perform, which was a problem I had going back to when I was seven years old in Little League. In the cult, I was called upon for various public speaking situations, such as teaching a group; leading meetings; and, worst of all, to give opinions at Elders' meetings. At the age of twenty-one, it was very intimidating to be among a group composed of lawyers, medical professionals, businessmen, a political leader, and others. Professionally, I had not accomplished anything at that time and felt like I was less than all the others. I managed to speak publicly when I had to, and I did it pretty well, though it took significant effort on my part to fight the phobia.

BCCI was a new and fascinating place to work. On my first day, I arrived early and waited in the hall for someone to arrive and open the doors to the office. Finally, a girl arrived and, in an abrupt tone, asked who I was. She was attractive, and I soon realized that all the women working there were very attractive. It was part of the successful image that the bank was trying to project: attractive employees and fancy offices in the Seagram Building located on Park Avenue a few blocks from the Waldorf Astoria Hotel.

The bank was still only a "representative office" while they awaited their full banking license in order to begin operations. I spent days just sitting around, talking to my boss, and studying materials. The pretty admins would walk around the office doing their work (which included serving coffee and tea, setting up lunches for the management, and cleaning up afterward). These were some tough New York City girls who did not appreciate the foreign culture they found themselves in. Yet the money was good, and that part of the city was enviable.

After a time, I bonded with several of them, as we were sort of cut from the same cloth in our backgrounds. We developed some very good friendships that helped us deal with and get by in that weird work environment.

CHAPTER 12

My Uncle and Me

During my two-week notice period at Chase, I had a good deal of free time. There was no internet back then, so, just for fun and to kill time, I grabbed a white pages phone book and started looking up people from my past.

I had wondered about my uncle, who had become a successful dentist and, last I heard, was living in Manhattan. I checked the phone book, and his name was listed under his practice that was located on 57th Street off Lexington Avenue, which was considered to be a high-class New York City area.

I hadn't seen or heard from him in the five years since we spoke briefly at my grandmother's funeral. He was very friendly as we spoke about the sadness of my grandmother's illness and passing. As we talked, I noticed the expensive suit he was wearing . . . and he looked great. As it was the last time I ever saw him, the memory of those few moments is still vivid.

It was another relationship my mother had destroyed. He was one of her two brothers—my uncles whom I was close to from infancy through the early teens. She would verbally rip him apart during her regular discussions with my father. They would sit in the living room sipping coffee and going around the horn, ripping everyone they knew to shreds. When it came to this uncle, she would go on about what a lousy dentist he was among the many other horrible things she would say about him.

Out of curiosity, I dialed the number, and a girl's voice said, "Dr. Green's office." I got nervous, not knowing how he would react to me, so I hung up. I figured I would catch up with him sometime later on, and I was happy that at least I knew where he was.

Around two weeks later, I was on my way home from work, walking up Langdale Street to our apartment. My wife was outside and told me she had some bad news, that someone in my family had died.

"Who, my grandfather?" I asked.

"No, your uncle," she replied.

My initial reaction was shock, as he was only forty-one years old and appeared to be in excellent physical shape. He had to take care of himself and watch his diet as a juvenile diabetic who was on insulin. Initially, we presumed that his diabetes had been the cause of or contributed to his death. The family had minimal contact with him in his adult life, and we were all sad and shocked. He was the first "professional" of the family, and we were all immensely proud of his accomplishments (with the exception, of course, of my mother).

Years later, one of my cousins who I reconnected with told me that he hadn't thought that Hal had any friends at all. He had wondered if anyone would even show up at his funeral. Although they were first cousins close in age and lived near each other, he never really got to know him. My cousin and his family called him a "phantom" because he would appear for a few minutes in Grandma's house and then disappear back into his room. He did not hang out with the family much, and the reason always given was that he was studying. My other uncle, Herb, who was Hal's and my mother's brother, had told me that his brother lived a very mysterious lifestyle.

My father drove us into Manhattan to attend the funeral at Riverside Memorial Chapel, located on the Upper West Side. I didn't think much when I saw several people standing outside, but, when I entered the building, the place was packed. When I realized all those people were there for my uncle's funeral, I was shocked. The people outside were the overflow from the crowd there to pay their respects to him.

My father told me he and a few other close family members were going inside to view the body with the casket open, and he asked if I wanted to join them. I thought about it for a minute and told him I didn't want to. My preference was to remember him the way he was when he was alive. Perhaps the memory of seeing my grandmother the day before she died looking like a human skeleton contributed to my decision. Regardless, I remain comfortable with that decision.

Seeing the considerable number of his friends there really piqued my curiosity as to my uncle's lifestyle. Before the service, I was sitting next to some guy on a bench in the lobby.

"He was my uncle," I told him, "but I hadn't seen him in many years. What was he like?"

He smiled and said, "He was a great guy . . . liked to party a lot."

I got the "great guy" part, but I wondered what "liked to party a lot" meant. The idea that my older uncle who was a dentist liked to go to parties seemed strange to me.

Following the funeral, all the talk started regarding what would happen with my uncle's estate. A few weeks later, I was asked to help clean out his apartment where he lived alone. For that first trip, me, my father, my sister's husband, and I drove into New York City to start the process. His apartment was located in a building on 86th Street between 2nd and 3rd avenues, which was a nice area.

We opened the door and walked into a mess; there were things strewn all over the place. Our task was to go through it all and determine if anything was worth keeping. I saw what looked like a nice stereo system, and underneath the turntable were albums and tapes. Going through his collection, I was surprised to see an Allman Brother's album, one of my all-time favorite bands, and another one by the Average White Band, who did funk type music. I started to get a glimpse into who he was through his music. There was a softer side revealed with Simon and Garfunkel, Buddy Holly, and Carly Simon. He had several books on a wide range of topics, from Einstein to sports figures and more.

I took home some of the tapes and books and was intrigued. It was reminiscent of when, as a child, I used to go through the boxes of his books and memorabilia in the closet of my grandparents' basement.

My brother-in-law and I were going through a hall closet and found a plastic bag that had some twigs and buds from weed. We also discovered the instructional wrapper you find with medications that tell you dosage and side effects, and this one was for Quaaludes. I knew what these were, and now some pieces were beginning to come together.

"Ludes," as they were commonly known, were quite popular and used by people in the discos during the '60s and '70s for a down, drowsy type of high. Cocaine was hugely popular in the '70s, and ludes were used to help people high on coke get to sleep. I was now getting a much different picture and understood what "liked to party" meant.

For some reason, the more I found out about him, the sadder I became. I deeply regretted that we did not have a relationship as adults. It was haunting me how we just missed each other by me not asking to speak to him when I called. I sensed there was something deeper going on, though I had no idea what it was.

I would get home from work and listen to his music, especially to the Carly Simon tape, and somehow feel a connection to him. Particularly the songs "Legend in Your Own Time" and "The Right Thing to Do" would just tear me apart.

I found out later on that he had dated a woman who was both a famous actress and a Playboy centerfold, traveled extensively, spent summers in the Hamptons, was a huge New York sports fan, and a music lover. I envied the lifestyle I thought he was living as opposed to mine.

Doing the unhealthy comparison thing, I felt that I had married too young. Money was tight, and I was bogged down with the financial responsibilities of having a wife and two young kids. Though we were from the same blood, it seemed that we were miles apart.

It did not make any logical sense why this was affecting me so deeply. I tried, but I could not stop feeling the emotional pain.

One day, during my lunch break at BCCI, my curiosity got the best of me, so I decided to take a walk on Lexington Avenue to find his office. It was a nice early spring day and I could hear the sounds of KC and the Sunshine Band song "Give It Up" coming out of the speakers of an electronics shop.

After the short four-block walk, I turned right on 57th Street and entered the building. I took the elevator up to the floor where his office was, and when I got off, I turned and saw "Dr. Hal Green" on the door, which hit me hard and made me incredibly sad. I wondered how, after achieving his level of professional success and the many friendships he enjoyed, he could be dead at such a young age. Losing family members and friends is always sad, though some hurt worse than others. This one hurt badly and left me with great sadness.

A series of strange events followed his death. The autopsy was performed by a friend of his who was a doctor, and the results of the report indicated that he had died from cardiac arrythmia. There was no mention of anything related to drugs, although cocaine use has been known to cause arrythmia. We speculated that perhaps his friend did not want the family to know anything about his drug use. This was all speculation, as a theory proposed by my mother on what killed him was that he went into a diabetic coma and fell, hitting his head. My aunt who saw him in the open casket told me years later that the gash on his head had her believing there was foul play involved. The unfortunate reality is that we will never know what actually happened to him.

A week or so later, we heard a report on the radio that two NYPD cops were arrested for stealing items from the apartment of a dead man who lived alone on the Upper East Side, and that dead man was my uncle. It was alleged that those cops knew a safecracker and used him when there was an opportunity to take advantage of a situation.

My uncle had a safe with gold coins worth a significant amount of money, and, along with other items, they mysteriously disappeared from the apartment. I'm not sure what ended up happening to those cops, but it was a hot news item for a day or two.

Another strange occurrence was when my grandfather contacted my parents in a panic. He had been approached by two goons where he hung out at a local car dealership, helping out there after he retired. They claimed my uncle owed them a large amount of money for drugs, and they wanted my grandfather to pay up. My mother, who would often conjure up her own version of things, thought that my grandfather must have opened his big mouth and some guys overheard him say that his rich dentist son passed away, so they saw an opportunity.

I also found out that the actress my uncle dated had been raped at the mansion of a famous movie producer who himself was mysteriously murdered a few years later. All these things raised many questions and suspicions. Was he really doing a lot of drugs and living a wild partying lifestyle? Was he involved with the wrong people, and could that have led to his death? We will never know the real story. The mystery of his life has followed him into his death.

I was haunted by all this for several months, and I can't recall ever reacting the same way to anyone else's death. I thought about how devastated my grandmother would have been if she was still alive at the time. It would have destroyed her, as she and other family members were so proud of him and his professional accomplishments. I did not understand my reaction until years later when I was going through some old pictures that my mother had given me. There I was at two years old, and my uncle, who was around twelve at the time, had his arm around me with a big smile on his face. Others show him holding me when I was an infant. He was like a big brother to me, and the fact that my mother had destroyed our relationship was heart-wrenching.

Many years later, when I reconnected with some relatives who were close to him, they provided me with some more insight into the mystery. That helped provide some level of comfort, but the full mystery will never be solved.

CHAPTER 13

Goin' Down the Road

The BCCI office moved from 375 Park Avenue across the street to the corner at 320 Park. The new office was beautifully constructed of Italian marble, with desks and other furniture made of thick mahogany. Beautiful plants were placed all around the general work area and in the conference rooms. Impressions were big for those folks, and the impressive office totally met that requirement.

I learned that the Pakistani culture is quite different from ours and that working for them could at times be very difficult. The American employees sort of bonded together, as we shared the frustrations of working in a very different culture and management style. We started to get together on Friday nights after work, which was a lot of fun as it helped to ease the pressures of the workweek.

It was all good fun, but I was somewhat conflicted. My wife was at home with our two young daughters while I was out partying, and several attractive girls were part of the group.

My manager had told me that once I earned my degree, I would have a good chance of getting a promotion and becoming an officer of the bank. Becoming an officer there was a big deal. You pretty much would have a job for life, could get a mortgage at a great interest rate, and receive big bonuses.

When I finally graduated, I requested a meeting with the general manager to tell him that I graduated. I told him that based on my degree and work performance, I had earned the promotion and should become an officer. He gave me some evasive BS, and I began to realize they would never make me an officer, as I wasn't one of them. I was really ticked off and decided that I needed to make a move. Within a few weeks, I was offered a position with the New York office of First National Bank of Chicago. I would start there as an officer with a better salary and a total compensation package.

My farewell party at BCCI was very emotional, as I had developed some good friendships with the people there, and I was feeling a sense of loss. I think that, subconsciously, the people there became a family. It was like the Turtle Guys when I was in high school and was saying goodbye to a family.

When one of my colleagues dropped me off at my car with all the gifts and cards from the farewell party, I broke down and cried as I drove away. I met with my ex-colleagues maybe two more times after I started my new job, but the thrill was gone. I decided after the last time that I would never go back, and I never did.

I started working at First Chicago, and it was very refreshing to be back in an American bank. My knowledge and experience continued to grow there, which ultimately led to my being sent to our Chicago head office to be part of a team that was evaluating vendor solutions for a new trade finance system. At that point, I started flying to Chicago almost every week, as that project led to a larger and more involved reengineering one. The experience I gained from working on those projects was significant and would ultimately help advance my career in a major way.

After graduating, I finally had some free time and was able to think about what I wanted to do next. I was driven to rectify things from my past that had gone wrong. One of the things that I loved as a young kid and had a passion for was music, in particular, the guitar. I had given it up after taking lessons when I was ten or eleven years old, thinking I didn't have it and just wasn't good enough.

It maybe seemed a little crazy, but I decided at the age of thirty-one to take up the guitar again. I started lessons with the son of the owner of a local music store in New Hyde Park. He was well trained and knowledgeable in jazz, classical, and, of course, rock music, which is what I was interested in. I spent a year with him, and it got me started on what would become a very long journey. I was hooked!

My love of guitar and my serious pursuit of it coincided nicely with my time in Chicago, the home of the blues. There were blues bars located throughout the city, and from the time I would get off the plane making my way to the taxi stand, there would typically be some guy playing great blues guitar.

One night, after a long meeting and dinner, the only people left were a consultant who used to live in Chicago and me. As we were out-of-towners, the only thing left to do after dinner was to go back to the hotel and watch TV. We were trying to come up with something to do, and I asked him if he wanted to go to a blues bar. He enthusiastically responded, "Yeah, I haven't done that in years!"

We pulled up in front of what looked like just a regular bar with a sign outside that read "BLUES." We entered the dumpy bar, and the band inside immediately caught my attention. The guitar player/singer was accompanied by drums, bass guitar, and a trombone player. They would be into a song when the lead guy would start telling stories before bursting into some amazing guitar playing. I was really enjoying it along with a diverse audience of everyone from older women to metal-head-looking young guys.

In my enthusiasm, I drank around seven screwdrivers and was feeling rather good. I headed to the men's room while the band was taking a break, and as I walked by them, I asked the lead guitarist if I could make a request.

"Sure," he said.

"'Red House,' it's an old Hendrix tune," I replied.

He told me they would be doing a little medley and would include that. I then foolishly told him, "And it's in B flat." I knew I made a mistake telling him that, but the alcohol made me do it.

After the break, he announced "We gonna do a little something now for y'all, and it's in B flat."

He proceeded to tear that song up while staring at me, and I gave him the thumbs up. It was all great fun. When I got home, I recalled that I had a guitar magazine that included a section called "Who's Who of Lesser-Known Blues Artists." I was thinking, *There's probably no way this guy is in here, but let me take a look.*

I turned several pages, looking at the various pictures and summaries, and then I could not believe it. There he was! His name was Maurice John Vaughn. He had two CDs out and had worked with Buddy Guy's brother Phil Guy, Son Seals, and other well-known musicians in the blues world. And there I was telling him a song was in the key of B flat!

That was one example of many great experiences I had while I was on the road for business and why I enjoyed entering the world of business travel. Another reason was because I never lived on my own before I was married, so it was like being on my own for the first time.

Typically, I would fly out on Sunday nights and return home Wednesday or Thursday. The excitement would begin upon entering a taxi outside of O'Hare airport where they had what was called "Share a Ride." If you shared the ride to downtown Chicago with one or two others, the rate would be split, which would help reduce company expenses.

What I really enjoyed was talking to the other passengers during the ride, as so many interesting people were arriving in town for various reasons. Some were there to attend science or medical conventions, while others were there for business purposes, and some just to visit relatives. I fully enjoyed my interactions with all those interesting and good people. Interacting with good people was something I loved, as it gave me hope to see and know that there is a lot of good out there in this world.

Even as a child, I always had a strong curiosity about other people and places. During our teenage years, Phil and I would dream about moving out of state and how much better life would be if we were living in Alabama or California. One of my fantasies back then was that I would move to California and get a simple, low-stress, secure job, like in the post office. After work I would come home to a loving wife, smoke some weed, and drink a little wine while relaxing to the sounds of the Grateful Dead.

What helped inspire that was John's older brother and sister, who took separate trips with friends cross-country in the summer of 1971. John's older brother Nick left New York permanently after a brief return from that trip. They all spent some time in Georgia before settling in California. Others around that time had also ventured off to other states, obsessed with leaving New York (which was decaying rapidly due to a major rise in crime, drugs, and poverty).

The garden apartment we were living in was not my cup of tea. It was noisy and had limited space for our family of four. Despite the experience I had gained, I found myself somewhat dead-ended and frustrated in my job. With the housing market going higher and higher in New York, it seemed that we were never going to be able to afford our own house in a decent neighborhood. On basically one income, we were getting nowhere. The combination of these things led Ann and me to start considering a move.

We had a slight hope that our apartment complex might go co-op, which was a growing trend in Queens. Several other complexes had already transitioned, and rumors began to spread that something was in the works with ours. Over several months of meetings with lawyers and other occupants, it actually happened. We had the option of taking a cash buyout, purchasing shares in the co-op for our apartment, or buying the right to purchase and then immediately selling those rights to another buyer. We chose to buy and sell our rights.

CHAPTER 14

Southbound

My old friend Andy, who years earlier had helped me get the job in freight forwarding, had already left New York, and, after a brief time in Georgia, he settled in Tampa, Florida. My brother-in-law's girlfriend, Lynn, had decided to take a buyout for her apartment in Floral Park, and they also had their sights set upon Tampa, where her parents were living after retirement.

It seemed to be in the cards that we would explore Tampa as our primary destination for relocation. We would fully think this out and do our homework in an effort to ensure that we would make a good decision. This was a big one, and we didn't want to screw it up.

We went on a goodbye tour of New York, part of which was a going away party with friends and some family members. I did not anticipate how poorly many of them would take it. At that time, Tom and Lynn had already moved down there, and we took an apartment in the same complex which was called the Altamonte. The plan was that we would blaze the trail, and, eventually, my mother-in-law, Mary, and her family would all move down there with us.

It seemed like a great plan; however, in looking back, some of it was based upon escapism, another coping mechanism in dealing with the pain from the abuse. Ann thought it would be good for us to have me relieved of the pressures from the New York rat race.

CHAPTER 15

Beauty's Only Skin Deep

*B*oth Ann and I were trying to escape for different reasons. Unknown to us at the time was that our relationship was troubled. Much of it was due to my problems from the abuse and hers from the abandonment by her father. One of my bosses used to say "problems don't age well." We learned that lesson from our long journey to Tampa and back.

One by one, things began to unravel. We had a nice apartment in what we initially thought was a good area. However, within a short period of time, we began to realize there was significant crime there and all around the area we were living.

My job prospects, which were good and well-thought-out prior to the move, were not happening for various reasons. It was going to take me longer than anticipated to get a job in my field and at the level I had achieved. Andy had made it clear that it might take him a little time to get me into Sun Bank, perhaps six months.

Around two weeks into this adventure, my mother-in-law started to complain about some medical issues. A brief time went by and then the dreaded diagnosis came: it was cancer. That sent my wife into a depression, as she was already not happy about the move.

Following a brief trip back to New York to visit my mother-in-law, we jointly came to the decision we wanted to move back home, though we wondered if that would even be possible. We started to plan a strategy, knowing that once we called our old bosses to see if we could get our jobs back, there would be no turning back.

One former employer I knew I wouldn't be calling was BCCI. Remember the friend who told me back in New York that BCCI was involved in laundering drug money? He was right. Ironically, BCCI was busted in a sting operation in Tampa while we were living there!

The toughest part of leaving Tampa was saying goodbye to Tom. He had been so happy that we were doing this thing together.

He followed us in his car to the main road for our journey home. As the cars separated, we were all in tears. The Tampa dream was over, and the next big challenge would be our return to New York.

CHAPTER 16

Brokedown Palace

*The palace filled with hopes and dreams
shattered and collapsed.*

The road back was long, though I was excited and happy to be going home. We had two cars, so we drove back separately. I knew Ann was hurting, but I believed that being back in New York would help her. She was terribly upset at what was happening to her mom, as the cancer was slowly killing her.

We finally made it over the Verrazano Bridge. After telling the family when we left New York that we would probably never again see that dirty, filthy, disgusting city, we were back on the Belt Parkway. It was a wild adventure for six months, and we learned many lessons, although many more challenges and lessons were on the road ahead of us.

John and Sue were living in a house and offered to let us stay with them until we could get resettled. The other option was to stay at my parents' house, which was big enough to accommodate us. However, I could not trust my parents, especially with our children. We mutually agreed that Ann and the kids would stay with John and Sue, and I would stay with my parents. I could deal with them alone, and there was a separate room and bath in the lower level of the house. It seemed like a reasonable temporary situation.

Coming home came with various challenges, the first of which was trying to find a new job. My old job with First Chicago Bank would eventually open up, though to rehire me at the same level would take some time. Ann got her old job back working for the doctor, but she was in a depression. I could always count on her to help face difficult circumstances jointly, and this was one of (if not the most) challenging circumstances we ever faced.

I would try to talk to her about what we needed to do and actions we needed to take. But, this time, things were different. I sensed she was far away and that she did not want anything to do with me. It got to the point that I asked her what was wrong. We had to make some important decisions, and we needed to work on these things together. She said that she could not deal with me right then and that I was too intense. Her mother and her mother's illness were all she could handle, so I and the other things would have to wait.

That really shook me up. Ann seemed to turn into another person. I felt like I was losing her and that our marriage was in serious trouble. All this was happening when I was in an extremely vulnerable position, perhaps more so than any other time in my entire life. We married when we were so young, and then we were wrapped up in the cult for the first nine years of our relationship. Many of the marriages that were in a comparable situation to ours had ended.

And, as if that weren't enough, I learned something that added even more to my insecurity and concern. I did some investigating and found out that one of the guys who she worked with in Tampa had been calling her when we got back to New York. She admitted to me that she was attracted to the guy, and I flipped out. I felt completely betrayed.

Ann's sister Mary was always a good friend and was someone I could talk to. When I told her what was going on, she talked to me almost every night, trying to help me understand that Ann was totally stressed out by her mom's cancer. That she was not herself and that she did still love me, and I needed to leave her alone for a while to allow her to get through it all.

I understood, though, that would be difficult for me as Ann had always been my rock. She would listen to me as I struggled through life with problems I did not know how to effectively deal with or why they were there. She could not be there for me during the very difficult situation we were in, and I had to face and accept that. I also began to understand and realize the many things I did not do well in our marriage that were contributing to Ann needing a break. I think we both needed that for different reasons.

I knew I needed to find a job in my field of work, but I decided to find something to make money and keep me occupied until that happened.

My brother had a friend whose brother had left the NYPD and started a limo company. I started driving for him, working nights and weekends. A job as a temp working for PNC Bank in New York became available, and they hired me. It was a foothold back into my field at a time when the job market was tight. My objective was to save as much money as possible so we could get our own place and restart our lives as a family again. I was highly motivated and worked like crazy.

Eventually, I was able to agree on a deal with my brother-in-law in which we would buy half his house, allowing him to move into a bigger house. It was not ideal, but it was another foot into another door. Partial ownership allowed us to eventually buy him out and have our own house in a place we had always wanted to be.

Going through the entire experience led to some serious introspection, and I thought it would also be a good idea for us to go for marriage counseling, something we had never done before. Although Ann was somewhat reluctant, she agreed.

We went to our first session with someone who was highly recommended. After the introductions, she had us meet with her separately.

At that point, I was starting to realize that my problems were having a major negative impact on Ann, though I did not know how to deal with them. Things like anger, anxiety, depression, and a phobia of public speaking had all plagued me. I blamed myself, as I could not figure out why I would get so nervous and fearful even expressing an opinion in a group meeting. I first started to become aware of that when I was an Elder in the cult. I had the same problem in work situations and wondered why. I also felt tremendous guilt that these problems were a burden for Ann and that it was all my fault that our marriage was in trouble.

Another aspect to it all was that, for years, I felt like a failure in my career. I knew I could do better than what I was doing, but I could not put it all together. To me, it didn't add up. I knew I was pretty smart and hardworking. I would often think that I was under some sort of curse that was preventing me from living up to my potential and having a satisfying and successful career.

The doctor and I started discussing how I was raised, my childhood, and my parents. I told her about the abuse, and she probed for more details, asking, "Were you ever hit?"

I told her I was.

Then she asked, "With objects?"

That question alone hit me hard. I immediately started to realize what was going on and the negative impacts of the abuse I had suffered.

Driving home, I was very surprised by that revelation and felt somewhere between depressed and relieved. I started thinking about how the abuse had impacted our marriage and how I viewed myself. It all started to make sense, and I was happy that at least the main problem was identified. It was a major turning point in our lives, as the road to recovery and healing had begun.

CHAPTER 17

Starting Over

*D*espite the epiphany regarding my abuse, we didn't really connect with that marriage counselor and stopped after a few sessions. However, the seed was planted. I felt I needed more.

I looked into my benefits and found that I could get five free therapy sessions. I chose a therapist somewhere in Queens, and, during the first session, he asked me what the main reasons were for my decision to move to Florida. I explained that the lifestyle appealed to me, and, that while we were scoping the place out, my brother-in-law had said, "This place is like a permanent Valium." After I said that, he repeated what I said and then wrote it down on his pad.

After the session, I asked myself why I was looking for that. I gave it more thought and realized that it was an escape mechanism. I was looking to escape from the pressures of family, young kids, money problems, job pressures, commuting daily, and living in an apartment I did not like. I wanted out, and I thought I could escape it all by moving. It didn't work out that way, and, upon our return, I just wanted stability in home, life, and work.

My mother-in-law passed away, which was a great loss for all of us in the family and for many others whose lives she had touched. Ann took it especially hard, which I understood. I remained sensitive to that and committed to doing everything I could to help her through her grief, including leaving her alone if that was what she needed.

A few months later, we were able to put together enough cash to consummate the house deal and move into our new house. Our dream to own a house in Nassau County, which had seemed impossible at the time we moved to Florida, had become a reality.

I worked one year at PNC and was promoted to supervisor. I liked it there. It was a small operation and the people were fun to work with. Ironically, soon after the promotion, my old boss at First Chicago called me and told me they were ready to take me back. It was a difficult decision, as the PNC people treated me well, but First Chicago was home, and I accepted the offer to return.

I now had a new job, a new house, and a very new outlook. Through the entire experience, I learned to appreciate the things I had, and not be upset about the things I didn't have, the old "glass half empty or glass half full" equation. I became much more sensitive to Ann's needs and focused more on the kids. I was thankful to be back at First Chicago and living in a place that was much better than any place we had lived in before.

Friends of ours who Ann had introduced me to a while back got in contact with us. They had gone through a similar experience to ours, having moved to North Carolina and then returning to New York. They were living close by, and we started spending time with them.

Ted had dabbled a bit on guitar and was a music lover, so I brought an acoustic to his house, and we played around on a few songs. He told me I needed to meet another guy who was the husband of one of my wife's coworkers. He told me that Tony was a great drummer and singer who also played some good guitar.

My wife went to a women's get-together at his wife Carmen's house, and even though I was invited, I declined. When Ann came home, I asked about the get-together and she told me that Carmen's husband Tony was there and that he played guitar and sang. I asked if he was good, and she said yes.

"How good?" I asked.

"He was just very good," she said.

Ted and his wife, Gianna, invited us over along with Tony and Carmen, which gave us the opportunity to meet them. After coffee, the three guys went into the living room, and we all played acoustics. Tony was like a jukebox, able to play all types of songs across genres, and meeting him was a game changer.

During the initial stages of learning how to play, I had jammed with a few guys. A colleague who I worked with at First Chicago was also trying to improve. He would come out from Harlem, where he lived with a few other guys, and we would jam at John's house. John played drums, and a sixteen-year-old son of a neighbor who was learning bass rounded out our fledgling band, which didn't last long. Tony had been in bands since he was a teen. He had played with guys in clubs and in big park concerts in Alley Pond Park that were sponsored by the Parks Department and took place weekly in the summertime.

At the time we met, he hadn't been playing with people for a while and liked the idea of getting together. One Saturday night, they invited us over, and I brought my electric guitar at his request. Another guy sat in on drums in an upstairs bedroom, and we jammed. Tony was really good; he had a great voice. He had also learned guitar by hanging around with the guitar players in the various bands he played in over the years. He loved the band Mountain and had a Leslie West-inspired style.

One day he told me that he found a tape of a band he was in back in 1971 while in high school. They sounded fantastic! He was on drums and the two guitar players were great. The lead singer, along with keyboard and bass players, rounded out the band. They were playing Allman Brothers' songs, and they really sounded like them.

One day at work I played the tape Tony found for a coworker and then played the Allman Brothers' version of the same song. My coworker wasn't familiar with the Allman Brothers' music, and when I asked him which version sounded better, he said the first one—which was Tony's band. That's how good they were. Just playing with him at our little social gatherings was helping to advance my playing.

We eventually formed a band that was not great, but it gave me my first experience playing a real gig in a bar. It was a big step up for me, as that was something I could only imagine doing when I first started to learn.

We played together for a few more years, with different guys moving in and out of the group. Interestingly, one of the guys we ran into was the lead guitarist from Tony's band back in high school. He was a bit rusty, having not played in years, but you could still tell how good he was. The bass player was another husband of a girl my wife knew from work. This guy looked like Sting as he walked into the basement of Tony's house one night. He played bass and knew a wide range of songs and could really sing. We played together for a year, but for several reasons, mostly to do with personalities, we dissolved it. However, it was another step up for me to play with some very talented guys.

After the breakup, Tony wound up playing drums in several local bar bands. I was happy for him but sad that we were no longer playing together. I understood that I was not on the same level, but it still hurt. But as one who no longer just gave up on things, I kept playing and trying to improve just for the love of it.

New CD stores were sprouting up everywhere, and this new form of digital music was taking over the music industry. One store, Uncle Phil's in Levittown, was where I would go to find CDs of some of my favorite classic rock and blues music. There was a kid working there who was friendly, and we would talk about music and guitars. In one of our conversations, he told me he had a great teacher who was located in Floral Park on the Nassau County side, which was just south of where I grew up. I asked him where he was from and he said Bellerose. He told me he had an older brother who had attended Martin Van Buren High School. I asked him what his last name was, and he said "Quartararo."

I was surprised and said, "I knew a guy in high school named Joey Quartararo."

"That's my older brother!" he said.

What a coincidence! Joey Q was also the lead singer from Tony's band in high school. Unbelievable!

Sometime later, Joey was visiting while in from California during Thanksgiving weekend, and the kid from the CD store arranged for a jam in a local studio. It was like a reunion of half the high school band, with Tony on drums, Rob on lead guitar, and Joey as the lead singer. His little brother John and I also played guitar, and another guy was on bass.

We played all kinds of different songs, from Allman Brothers to Stevie Wonder. Joey was amazing, showing he still had it as a frontman lead singer. We had a fantastic time, and I was honored to be a part of it.

Joey looked quite different than the guy who was ahead of his time in the way he dressed and carried himself in high school. Back then, he would come into the bathroom between periods, where we would all be smoking cigarettes. He would make his way around smiling and asking how everyone was doing. We would all just look at each other and shake our heads, but it was hard not to like the guy. He had a big smile and was filled with energy.

That night after the jam, he walked with me to my car. He no longer had the same look; he was very thin and drawn, and I could only wonder what life had done to him. He thanked me for coming down for the jam and said he recognized me from my smile and how I was always smiling when we were kids. As I drove home, I was on cloud nine after what felt like a peak experience. Yet I wondered how I could have always been smiling back then despite all my pain.

I asked John from the CD store more about his guitar teacher, and he told me his name was Larry. He mentioned that he had a notebook from his lessons with Larry and that he would let me borrow it.

As I started going through the pages of handwritten notes, charts, and diagrams, I realized that this guy Larry seemed to get right to certain points. I had been struggling to learn some things, and it looked like he was covering exactly what I was having difficulty with.

When I called Larry to set up a lesson, he asked me what kind of music I liked, and I told him mostly classic rock and blues. Allman Brothers and Grateful Dead were at the top of the list of what I wanted to learn. He told me I was going to love the lessons.

I arrived at a house that from the outside looked a little creepy, as it was old and had overgrown shrubbery in the front. I double-checked the address to make sure I was in the right place, and I was. I went to the front door and rang the bell (which apparently wasn't working as I saw two elderly people walking around and not reacting to the bell). I knocked on the door several times, to no avail.

I figured I would give it another try. I went into the backyard, hoping I wasn't going to get arrested if this was the wrong house.

The elderly man opened the door, and I asked him if a guy named Larry lived there. "Sure, come on in," he said. He opened a door to the basement and yelled, "Larry, someone is here to see you."

On the phone, Larry had sounded very conservative, so that was the image that formed in my mind. When the door swung open, I saw this guy with long reddish-blond hair and a thick, full beard.

"You're a little early," he said, "but come on downstairs."

The unfinished basement was filled with all sorts of old amplifiers and guitars everywhere. In the middle of the room was an old beat-up sofa with two guitars lying on it and a chair set opposite. A small, old, black-and-white TV was beside the sofa on top of a table in front of which was an ashtray filled with cigarette butts.

Larry's first words were "Why are you here?"

I explained how I had started playing seriously later in life than many of my friends who played. How I wanted to develop and improve my playing and needed to learn some blues and rock techniques that I was not yet getting.

"Okay," he said. "Let's start here."

He started writing in the notebook he told me to bring, and, from there, we took off.

The year that followed was life-changing. In addition to being a great player, Larry was also a great teacher. He knew exactly what I needed to learn in order to improve, and he had the ability to communicate in a way that I could comprehend. The result was that the foundation laid by Larry helped my playing improve significantly. My love of music and playing the guitar led to years of fun, many interesting interactions playing with other people, and being in a few bands. Playing guitar became my favorite hobby and eventually became my passion.

During our lessons, I also got to know Larry as a person, and sometimes we would talk about things other than music, like sports and politics. I describe Larry as a hidden treasure: eccentric, brilliant, and someone who really cared about people. He could have been somewhere in the limelight musically, but, for whatever reason, he chose to teach numerous students in his unfinished basement.

When the year was up, I felt I had learned enough to take it forward on my own, at least for a while. After covering the basics of classic rock, blues, country, and some slide and bass guitar, I had plenty to chew on. I thought that at a later point I would go back and focus on jazz, flamenco, or some other genre. Larry would be there to help me go on to some great new aspects of playing.

A few years later, I heard that he had unfortunately passed away after a battle with cancer. He was a man who lived his life against the grain and touched many other lives in the process.

One of his friends set up a page on Facebook to honor Larry, and I was amazed to see all the stories there regarding how he had impacted so many lives. It is as if the lessons were a vehicle to go beyond the music and into meaningful relationships with his students.

Every year, on his birthday, people post stories, pictures, video, and audio recordings of him. He truly is forever in our hearts.

CHAPTER 18

You Have a Good Life

After the crazy Florida adventure, I craved stability in our lives. Thankfully, that was finally starting to take shape. We were in a nice house, had our jobs back, and my guitar hobby led me to some new talented people to play with. I appreciated my job more than I had previously and became more interested in my field of trade finance. Things at the bank were good, and I was made a supervisor of a small unit. However, a major change took place that led to something new and exciting.

Having previously spent time in the Chicago head office, I was chosen to participate in a major reengineering project. Consultants were hired and brought in to evaluate all aspects of the department and make recommendations to increase profitability. I wasn't sure exactly why I was chosen, and there was some resentment from a few within the New York office regarding that. I later found out that Mick Berg, the department senior manager who had always liked me, had requested that I be included. I was also being mentored by Felicia, our sales manager, and I think they both saw more potential in me than I did in myself.

In later years, we would cross paths and almost ended up working together a few times. I appreciated both of them help me rise to higher levels and advance my career.

I was entering a whole new world in which I would be working mostly in Chicago and traveling there almost every week. I started to meet a new set of people and became extremely interested in what the consultants were doing and how they operated. Their model allowed them to live anywhere in the US or Canada, arrive at the location by noon on Monday, work heavy hours Tuesday through Thursday, and leave for home Friday at noon.

Most importantly, I began to learn new skills of business analysis related to operations, sales, marketing, investment, costs, and more. It was the first time I became acquainted with laptop PCs, which is what the consultants were using for presentations and spreadsheets. It was all new and exciting, and I felt that I was part of something that would be looked back on historically as a turning point in the business world. I told Ann that I sensed this would lead to something better for me after the project, though I did not know exactly what that would be.

My old friend Andy had moved on from the bank and started an export services company that provided a range of services and consulting for our banking clients. It was a perfect match, and we at the bank were working with his company.

One day, it hit me that as I was already selling his services to our clients, perhaps I could move into working for him full time. We came to an agreement, and I decided to be bold. Taking a big chance, I made the move.

It turned out to be one of those fateful decisions that would change the course of not only my career but also of the rest of my life.

My involvement in the business lasted two years before I decided to move on. My time there afforded me the opportunity to focus on hard-core sales: if I didn't sell, I didn't make money.

It also gave me the chance to learn more about computer hardware and software. I had to set up a network in my home office to accommodate the people working for me and to connect with the office in Atlanta. I was intrigued with the programming Andy had done to develop the software we used for preparing various export documents. I would spend hours after the workday teaching myself the basics of programming, and I tried to duplicate the existing code in a more advanced language.

I began to realize the potential of what could be done with code, and that really excited me in a way like nothing other than music and learning guitar ever had. My brother-in-law, who would help me out in my new pursuit, told me that I should keep doing what I was doing, that it had real-world value. I didn't believe him, as I was interested in it only as a hobby and had no formal training.

The business was progressing well, and I was able to build up a solid customer base of freight forwarders and exporters. I hired a few people to work part time, allowing me to devote more time to sales and overall management.

Unfortunately, some unexpected things arose that had me rethinking if I wanted to keep it going or not. Andy's wife was getting more involved in the business, and I didn't think that was a good idea, though I had no say in the matter. He was also expanding into an area of the business that I thought was questionable. During my reevaluation, I also had to face the reality that the income was not worth the time and effort I had to put into it. I made the difficult decision to end my relationship with the business and close down my office.

The combination of skills that I acquired in those two years would lead me to the next leg of my journey, something I never would have expected. It took me two years to build up the business and a few days to dismantle the home office. It was very depressing, and I cried my eyes out as I looked around at the empty office. All the work, crazy hours, and the good people who worked with me were gone. However, that old Buddhist principle would soon prove itself once again.

After closing it all down, I had to determine what my next step would be. I asked myself what I enjoyed doing the most from all my previous work, and the answer was sales and technology. I was always told by people that I should be in sales, and now technology was my newfound hobby. I really didn't think that I had the educational background for a job selling technology, but I started to explore that.

To my surprise, I came across an ad in which a company was looking for someone with trade finance banking, sales experience, and some knowledge of software. That led to a good interview, and the company loved my experience. However, the compensation was not what I needed, even though it would increase over time. The important thing was it showed me that the skill set I had developed did have value and could lead to working at things I really enjoyed doing.

A few weeks later, I received two offers and decided to join a company that had been providing trade finance software solutions to banks for several years. It was the start of my new career, one in which I could finally reach my potential doing what I enjoyed most.

Over the next several years I worked for two other information technology (IT) companies and a few years at a bank in a technology-related position. Over the course of that time, I succeeded in a variety of positions across sales, operations, and product management. I served the industry well and earned the respect of my peers. As one former colleague of mine from one of the IT companies once said to me, "We worked hard, had a lot of fun, and made a lot of money. If only it could *always* be that way."

Things were good, and I was filled with excitement and enthusiasm when I was working on a sales deal with a major US bank located in Boston. It was a grueling year-long process, and we had finally been selected as the vendor of choice.

During that time, I was introduced to a very bright software developer named Brad who had built a front-end component that would integrate to our back-end process-ing system. We immediately hit it off; I just liked the guy.

Though he was probably the smartest developer I ever worked with, he was very down to earth. He explained that he had a small company, and they eventually wanted to sell their product to other banks. When I heard that, the light bulb turned on, and I thought that would be a fantastic opportunity.

The big deal I had been working on fell through when we were in contract negotiations as the bank was suddenly acquired by another bank. I became disillusioned and thought about contacting the owner of that company who had built the front end. He responded to my email and asked if I was ready to move to Colorado, where he was located. I wasn't going to do that, but we agreed to a remote working situation.

Working in that small company and with that team was fantastic. I was the sales manager, and, as a team, we had enormous success. When Brad hired me, he told me that he was going to sell the company to a larger company and asked if I was on board with that. I told him I was, and even though I was very new to the company, Brad included me in some stock options, which was a pleasant surprise when the sale was concluded.

The new company we were sold to was headquartered in Atlanta—a very different world from what I was used to. I reported into an office located in Charlotte, North Carolina, and it could not have been more different from the Asian-based company where I had started my IT career. The company employed a high concentration of people who were from the South, and many were highly educated at some top universities. The Asian company had people from all over the world: Asia, Europe, and the Middle East. These were obviously vastly different cultures.

Working for the Asian company was when I started traveling internationally. My first flight was fourteen hours from JFK airport in New York direct to Tokyo. In addition to Japan, I spent time in Singapore, Hong Kong, and a month in the Philippines. Several cities in Europe, Latin America, and a week in Dubai rounded it out. I had absolutely amazing experiences spending time in all those places, working and interacting with people from diverse cultures.

The culture and people who worked in the new company in North Carolina were quite different. I was readily accepted; however, it was an adjustment, as I was coming from a whole different place. The main thing that helped me earn credibility was succeeding at my job. Several of the people working there were highly experienced in all aspects of the information technology business. They had more formal training and experience than I did, but I was fully determined to learn and succeed. Despite the big adjustment, I was able to adapt, and it became probably the best working experience I ever had.

I sometimes wonder how this guy from Brooklyn and Queens who had such a tough upbringing was now among an exceptionally talented and experienced team of people in a very interesting and challenging industry. I often told my daughters that whenever they see an opportunity, they should seize it. That's what I always did, and though the road was long and hard, career-wise, it paid off very well.

I'm Just Like You

Working in the IT business had me in a challenging, fast-paced competitive environment in which some old demons began to resurface. In the midst of my success, I had some self-doubts and wasn't sure why that was happening. I would still sometimes get nervous when I had to speak publicly even though I was a decent speaker. I had a general feeling that I still wasn't good enough or doing a good enough job. Comparisons would have me thinking that I wasn't as good as some of my colleagues, a similar pattern to how I felt regarding the people from back in Queens who went on to very successful careers. If I sensed that someone was judging me in that way, I would get upset and angry. It hit a point in which I decided to look into therapy again and continue beyond the few brief sessions I had participated in several years prior. Something still wasn't right and I was determined to find out what it was and deal with it.

I started by checking the list of approved providers in my medical plan, someone local and preferably Jewish.

Right or wrong, I felt that in order for a person to truly understand my conflicts, it would have to be a Jew. I tried several names from the list and left several messages with the various ones I found. Finally, one of them called me back, so we set up an appointment at his nearby office. I'll refer to him as Dr. K.

When we met for our first session, I liked him, and we had a good discussion. I gave him an overview of why I was there by explaining the child abuse and trauma I had endured. I told him about my family, marriage, and job, and how even though things had improved in my career and life in general, I still felt like something was not right.

He seemed interested and intrigued that someone coming from the childhood I had could turn out "okay." He explained to me that compared to many of the patients he had over the years, I now had a good life. That really struck a chord, and as I drove home, I kept repeating in my mind, *I have a good life.*

Yes, I reiterated to myself, *he's right. I really* do *have a good life.*

That was the beginning of the great work Dr. K did for me. I researched him a bit and was surprised that a random phone call from a list of providers would lead me to someone who had such a distinguished career.

One of his specialties was adoption and its impact on the children who were adoptees. Related to that expertise was what is known as forensic psychology. That led him to testify at several famous trials in which the defendants who were mostly serial killers were adoptees. He had run a clinic at one time and was quoted in other books on the subject of adoption. He was highly credentialed and experienced, which gave me a strong degree of confidence that he was the right person to help me.

In subsequent sessions, he explained that he wasn't big on categorizing diagnoses of his patients. He also wasn't big on medication; his approach was based on "cognitive behavioral therapy," which helps patients change their thinking pattern about things past and present.

I had sensed that certain things from my childhood had been affecting me at work and with my family and friends. I didn't know the cause or how to manage and overcome what was plaguing me. We covered a wide range of topics, and a core issue was how certain situations would subconsciously set off reminders of my mother's abusive treatment, particularly when she would be comparing me negatively to others.

One major problem was that I reacted emotionally when being compared to others. I could always deal fairly well with competition, and, in many cases, I would thrive in competitive situations. However, when someone else was being praised or lauded (especially if it was undeserved), it would sometimes set off terrible feelings within me. Much (if not all) of this was my own perception and not reality.

One example of this occurred one day while I was having a heart-to-heart discussion with one of my bosses, someone I liked and had tremendous respect for. I had been considering retirement a bit earlier than anticipated. When he asked why, I told him I felt like I was being pushed out of my job. I felt that way because a colleague who had recently been hired was receiving a good deal of attention from my immediate boss, and I was then being left out of new and interesting work that I had initiated. My boss was very perceptive, and the main thing that hit me was when he said, "It's all in your head, Rory."

After our discussion, I decided to stay on the job a few more years. I told Ann about it and she agreed with him. She had a good understanding of this problem and said she felt sorry for me because despite a highly successful career, these underlying issues detracted from the enjoyment and pride I should have been experiencing from my accomplishments.

The therapy sessions helped me develop an understanding of how several emotional reactions I was having in the present were not rational; they stemmed from things that happened to me in childhood.

My mother, in her fits of rage, would run off a list of all the things she thought I was bad at or had done wrong. Hearing that as a kid over and over led me to believe that I was no good, crazy, and less than others. Those scars run deep, and I read about how they have destroyed many lives by leading to low self-esteem and major addiction problems.

The long-term impacts the abuse had on me created an anger that resulted in rebellious behavior that was beyond what would be considered "normal" teenage rebellion. It resulted in the many street fights I had while growing up.

Another major issue was the guilt and sense of failure I had about leaving my early childhood friends who were Jewish. My mother would question why I was not hanging around with those kids anymore and would try to make me feel guilty about it. Most of my friends in high school were Italian and Irish, and I always felt more comfortable with them.

Later in life, when I got married young and we were struggling financially, I would hear about those Jewish friends who went directly to college. Several had become successful doctors, lawyers, and businesspeople. For years I felt like I had made a big mistake by not staying on a steadier path and going to college right away. I thought my life would have been so much better had I done that, but I later realized it was just a delusion.

In the sessions with Dr. K, we addressed those core issues, and, over time, he helped me understand why I was troubled. Just understanding those things helped diffuse the negative effects they were having on me and my life. It was reshaping the way I thought about those things and seeing the more positive aspects of my history.

For example, when I struggled in the SP program and was ultimately removed from it, I thought I was a failure and not very smart. Dr. K told me about that program, as he had some experience with a similar program. He explained that I had to be pretty smart to even make it into the program, which required an IQ of 130 or higher. I was walking around thinking I was not very smart when, again, it was all in my head.

When we discussed the friends I had left, Dr. K told me that I didn't really know them as adults and who they truly were as people. He referred to them as "paper people," which really hit home. I had some contrived ideas as to what they were like and how they were doing, but, again, it was all in my head. I thought they were all living wonderful happy lives, but I learned later that nothing could be further from that. They all had and have their own sets of problems and challenges, as most people do.

This was an especially important development in my recovery. Those feelings ran deep and were tied to my parents and early childhood in my grandmother's house in Brooklyn. Dr. K asked me if I could talk to the paper people today what I would say to them. It was one of the few times I broke down in the sessions when I responded, "I want to be just like you."

Around a year later, I heard that the wife of one of the paper people, who I will refer to as Dr. G, had been tragically killed in a car accident by a drunk driver. It was announced on the radio and in a local newspaper. I had known this friend since the third grade, and we were in many classes together during elementary school. We began to drift apart in high school, after which he went on to become a remarkably successful doctor. We hadn't seen or spoken to each other since shortly after high school, though we had been very good friends when we were young. Among other activities, we constantly played basketball and went to a few Knick games together.

When I heard that terrible news, I felt sorry for him and wanted to go see him. I strongly felt that I should be there to show support.

Initially, I was somewhat hesitant because I wasn't sure how I would be received after us being estranged for so many years. I gave it some serious thought and finally decided that I would go to his house and pay my respects. I hoped that would perhaps help him in some small way to deal with his grief.

I pulled up to the house, and there he was, in the driveway, heading toward the house. I reintroduced myself, and he gave me a big hug. He introduced me to all the people in the house and proudly told them how we had known each other since the third grade.

Among the other mourners was another guy whom I had been close to from our group of friends in the early days. He had become a successful businessman, and, as a kid, I knew his family well. His mother in particular was always genuinely nice to me, and his older brother taught me how to play basketball on the court in his backyard. He was also extremely glad to see me.

As I drove home, it was like I was in a dream. I knew Dr. G would be all right after the tragedy. I could just sense it from the way he conducted himself as his nephew read scripture and spoke about the woman of the house creating a light. How the light his wife had already created would continue to shine in him and his three sons.

I was told that I had just missed another friend who was there earlier that day. It was my good friend Ari, whom

I first met in the second grade and hadn't seen since high school. He had become a successful attorney and had an office in Manhattan.

We met for lunch a brief time later, and when we sat down at the table, he said, "So tell me what you have been doing for the past forty years."

We talked for over two hours, catching up on everything, after which he said to me: "I still like you."

I was ecstatic that I had somehow reconnected with the paper people who now became real people again. It meant so much to me to get to know them again. In the process of our renewed friendships, I was able to understand that their lives were not all picture perfect like I had imagined them to be. Shattering that illusion was very eye-opening and helpful.

Ari even convinced me to go to our fortieth high school reunion, which was the first school reunion I ever attended. I was glad I decided to go and didn't feel like I was less than anyone there because I knew that I wasn't.

The effects of childhood trauma never fully go away, but therapy can help immensely in learning how to manage them effectively. The reconnections and, to some extent, the high school reunion revealed to me that, in some ways, I am just like them, but in many ways, I am not. What happened to me as a child sets me apart, but the connections we made at a young age still remain in a very meaningful way, and, to this day, we are very good friends.

Dr. K told me that one major reason I was able to survive and later thrive in life was due to those and other connections. The people from the neighborhood, friends, and some of their families were major contributors. It was instinctive to develop those relationships as a survival mechanism, and I will always deeply appreciate all of them. That those bonds still remain after all these years is something very special.

∽

My career was thriving when I took on a position with a bank in Cleveland that required me to learn a related yet different side of the business. I knew it would involve heavy travel, and, at the time, I liked that idea. I developed a routine that included having a steady driver to and from the airport in Cleveland and staying at a unique Hyatt Hotel® that the bank used. I was there so often, it started to feel like going there was like going home. The work was challenging, and my boss who recruited me was tough but very smart and knowledgeable in all aspects of the business. He was a great mentor, and I fully enjoyed learning about and meeting the many challenges we faced together while working there.

After two years with the bank, I thought I would have a solid future there, so I decided that I would hang my hat there for the long term.

Suddenly, the crash of 2008 came about, and everything changed. The bank was acquired by PNC Bank in Pittsburgh, and the uncertainty was upon all of us at National City Bank. Seven months into the transition, my boss and I were told we would be "replaced." I was told I had to stay on for seven more months to help with the integration project before my exit. Fortunately, I had an exceptionally good severance deal in place.

Two weeks after my exit from the bank, and after much internal struggle regarding what direction I wanted to go, I decided to rejoin my former IT company. We remained in close contact, and my bank even bought and successfully implemented their trade finance system. It was as if I was still working with them from another side.

My return worked out very well financially, and I was given a good deal of flexibility to help grow the business. I started to participate in webinars and panel discussions, sales went very well, and the product was continuing to advance as an industry-leading one. I was traveling to Europe and Asia, working with our people in those regions to help them sell the solution. Singapore, Germany, England, Spain, The Netherlands, and Austria were incredible places that provided me with unforgettable experiences.

While that was all going very well, out of nowhere, I was told that our old neighborhood would be having a reunion. It was to be with my old high school crowd, the Turtle Guys, and would take place in Alley Pond Park, where we hung out so many years ago. When Phil asked me if I was going, I told him I didn't want to. I was living in a vastly different world and thought that I had nothing in common with those people anymore. What would be the purpose?

The night before the reunion, Phil pressed further. "Come on," he said. "You'll eat a few burgers and play a little acoustic with Cappy." (Cappy was a guy I knew a bit back when we were teens, though he got more involved with the group after I left.)

I told Phil I would think about it, and when I did, I thought, *Yeah, he's right.*

Previously, those reunions would draw maybe ten people, but I decided to go for a day in the park. I heard Cappy was a good guitar player and thought that maybe we'd get to play a few songs together. At the time, playing with others was not something I could do very often with the demands of my job, so it all seemed like a good idea.

An event that initially I did not want to attend turned out to be amazing. Many people I had not seen since high school were among those who showed up. I found it incredible to see one after the other. Guys and girls came walking up to the picnic area where it was set up. It was very emotional for me to see so many friends I had from when we were growing up, and I even had great conversations with some who I never spoke to back in the day.

At one point, I looked around at the park and had a strange feeling as I realized that this was the place where I had spent so much time hanging out as a teen. Now, on that day so many years later, I was back there after living my adult life, being married with children, and having an interesting, challenging career.

A few hours into it, Cap asked me if I wanted to play some acoustic guitar, and I agreed. We had never played together, so we just asked each other if we knew a song, and if we both did, we would play it.

In the middle of playing "Friend of the Devil," I noticed a few people singing along. I had always wished I could play in front of those friends, and, after a very long road, I was there doing it. We received several compliments after we finished playing, some even asking us how long we had played together. It was great and the beginning of several more performances with Cappy that would take place later.

When I got home, Ann asked me how it went.

"It was one of the best days of my life," I replied.

She laughed, as she knew well my tendency to complain about going to certain places, only to wind up having a great time.

This gathering at Alley Pond Park made me start to think about how much those people who showed up meant to me, the ones I thought I had nothing in common with anymore. Those teen years were times of great turmoil for me, yet the friends I had were there for me and had my back through it all.

I started to question where I was with regard to my career. The demands and pressures were so great, and I wondered how much longer I wanted to continue in it. A seed was planted that day.

The next big event was what we called a "Turtle Reunion" that occurred as a result of the unexpectedly large turnout at Alley Pond Park. One of the Turtle Guys, Paulie, was a guy I had known since I was fourteen years old when we were on the same baseball team. At the gathering, he said he wanted "to have it bigger and better" the following year at his house.

Preparations for the following year started soon after the Alley Pond reunion. I met with Cappy at his house to get to know each other better as adults and to talk about music. He was someone who played quite a bit with a variety of other musicians and was very good and knowledgeable.

During the first meeting, we wound up mostly talking about neighborhood memories and old friends. That led to us meeting a few months later when the plans for the big party were being formed. At that time, we decided that there would be two bands, and we would open. The headliner was a band called "Pa Creek," which had been the house band for many of the Turtle parties that took place after I left the group years prior.

I recruited my godson and nephew (who was an excellent all-around musician) to play drums. We had Cappy on bass guitar, me on lead, and we needed one more guitar player.

Paulie contacted me and asked if he could play a few songs with us, and we agreed. I had been to many backyard gatherings over the years when if a band was playing and their set was over, they would ask other players to come up and jam on a few songs. I had no issue with it as I was anticipating a loose backyard barbecue environment. Once we started to get together to practice, it morphed into the four of us to play ten songs as the opening band.

After only three and a half months of practice, we were ready to go. The energy was great that day, which started when we met early to set everything up. Woody was the leader of the other band, and I had been told that he had enough equipment to play Madison Square Garden. I thought it was a joke, but the guys said they were serious.

Woody and I were only acquaintances from back in the day and really only got to know each other through the process of setting this all up. We hit it off well and, after the reunion party, developed a great friendship. He's a unique and very smart guy in many different areas, including music and electronics related to guitars and equipment. It's been a great friendship that only developed at this later stage of life with an old neighborhood guy.

To accommodate everything, Paulie had a small stage built, and he hired a guy to videotape it all. What I thought would be a small, informal barbecue turned out to be around two hundred people from the old neighborhood. It was just incredible. Some of the people who showed up I forgot even existed!

The only downer was that the party followed the unexpected death of one of our guys a week prior who died unexpectedly. His nickname was "Red," and he was just a good guy who loved to have a good time. I had played basketball with him, his brother, and cousins often during our teen years, and he was damn good. It was sad, especially because he had really enjoyed the previous reunion at Alley Pond. We honored him with a moment of silence before the party got underway.

We played our ten songs, and, though it wasn't perfect, the crowd really appreciated it. Many people complimented us and really enjoyed seeing their friends up there tackling a wide range of songs from Grateful Dead, Allman Brothers, Stevie Ray Vaughn, and others. The high note was our last song: "Whipping Post," the classic Allman Brothers tune. Although it may have been the most difficult number, we seemed to play it better than the others. My nephew killed it on the drums, and we all did well.

The dream from so many years ago, to be playing in front of those friends, had become a reality. I thought about that a few times as we were playing, especially during "Whipping Post." I and many others commented in the days that followed what an amazing experience it was. Dr. K coined it as a "peak experience," and it was truly one of the best days of my life.

CHAPTER 19

Best Day, Worst Day

*A*round the time when preparations were being made for the party, I received a call from my sister to tell me that my father was in the hospital again. He had been there many times in the years prior due to various ailments. He was from the old school, in which going to a doctor and heeding their advice was not what many people did. He paid the price for mostly ignoring his various illnesses.

I debated what, if anything, to do, as I hadn't spoken with my parents and siblings for several years after deciding that it was in my own best interest to keep my distance. My father had called me when I first cut off contact, and I explained why. He understood and had no good answers regarding my question as to why he never did anything to stop the abuse, especially that which came from my mother. I told him I would think about his request to reconsider my position.

When he called, I had been listening to the Beatle song "And Your Bird Can Sing," and, as a result, when I hear that song now, I think about him and that phone call.

After much internal struggle, I decided I would visit him in the hospital. We had a good visit, and that was the last time I ever saw him.

Two weeks after the peak experience of the Turtle Reunion, I received a letter from my mother. When I opened it, I saw it was from a memorial chapel and laughed while asking Ann, "Is my mother trying to get me to buy a burial plot?"

Ann looked at the letter and said, "Your father died, that's what this is."

He had died two weeks earlier, and I was never told. Ironically, it was the same day as the Turtle Reunion.

A few months later, I decided to visit his grave, which was very emotional and sad. When I saw the words "Proud Poppa" on his headstone, it hit me that he did love his grandchildren and that he did, in fact, have a heart.

I uttered the words, "Somehow, it all went wrong."

Their problems were too big for them to solve without help that they would never have sought. When I walked from the grave to my car and sat down, it all hit me. I was overcome like never before and never since. I wailed uncontrollably for quite a while until I could compose myself and go home.

CHAPTER 20

My Girls

My daughters are both quite different from each other. Eleanor, our first born, had her time of normal teen rebellion and was into the scene of artsy type people, their appearance, and music. My younger one, Fran, was more into fashion and hung out with the kids from the more affluent sections of our neighborhood, like South Bellmore and Merrick.

When Fran graduated from junior high, I asked Eleanor about the diverse types of kids in high school. She explained things about the nerds, jocks, freaks, and rich snobs. I asked her how Fran would get along with the rich, snobby ones from the south side of town. She responded, "Dad, Fran *is* one of those kids."

Both girls were very smart, and I strongly encouraged them to go to college right away for at least two years. I explained how that would help them if they later decided they wanted or needed to go back to school, as they would already have two years completed. Eleanor was making her way after high school by taking some classes and working in different jobs. Fran wanted to go to school in California, which Ann was totally against. Fran and I discussed why she wanted to go there, and she made a solid case that sold me.

A few days before she left, we had lunch in a local diner. I told her that this would be an opportunity for her but that she needed to maintain her grades or else we would not continue to pay for her to stay. She agreed, and I felt a great sadness and fear of her leaving home and going out on her own.

We heard the Dave Matthews song "Where Are You Going?" on the ride back home from the diner, and that was our song. Every time I heard that song when she was gone, it would haunt me and bring on sadness.

Eleanor had a boyfriend who was an exceptionally talented tattoo artist, and, although not my thing, I remained open-minded. All her artsy friends and their ways were a bit foreign to me, but they seemed harmless. My daughter appeared to be stable, and I had confidence she would go through the various stages of life and wind up okay.

I was more concerned about Fran. We always got along well, and she was a happy child who seemed to take everything in stride. Eleanor was always in my face, knowing how to push my buttons to get me angry.

Fran did well and maintained good grades for the first one or two semesters. I had a business trip to LA and arranged it so that I could visit her at school for the weekend in Santa Barbara. That visit is memorable, as it coincided with the outbreak of the second war in Iraq.

People at my job were extremely nervous, as was I, regarding what was happening. When I arrived and spent some time at the apartment where Fran was living, I started to wonder how much of the time there was focused on school versus partying. The plan was that she would attend the community college and attain the necessary grades to then enroll at the University of California, Santa Barbara, which was a decent school.

On my last day there, we went to the beach and a state park, and the kids seemed oblivious to the war and the dangerous situation our country was in. We drove through an area near the beach in the late afternoon, and the kids who lived there were setting up speakers on their decks facing the street for the evening party. My daughter said, "Dad, you have to come here tonight . . ."

I told her that would not be happening. I just had a bad vibe about the whole scene out there and left feeling genuinely concerned.

My wife and I visited again a few months later, and Fran had a different boyfriend than the guy I met during my first visit. We all went to dinner, and he seemed okay, so I didn't think too much about it. He turned out to be a nut, and that relationship went south rapidly.

On a subsequent business trip, I was in a hotel in San Francisco when Fran was at this guy's house somewhere off campus. I received a panicked phone call from her. She had no money to get back to campus, and he was refusing to give it to her. I was able to work it out, but I wanted to beat the shit out of that jerk. That was one of what would become an increasingly large number of calls regarding all sorts of problems going on out there. Her grades had gone down after that first semester, so we pulled the financial plug and she finally had to return home.

We were all extremely disappointed that things did not work out. However, Fran is probably the most resilient person I have ever known. Following that major disappointment, it was a long road back, but she made it. She went through hell on that adventure but "worst thing is the best thing" readily applies here.

In the years that followed, she pulled her life back together, and I was excited when one day she told us she was pregnant, though I was also somewhat concerned about her health due to her seizure disorder.

One day during her pregnancy, I was awaiting Ann's return home from work for us to go to a show on Broadway in New York City. I heard a loud bang and thought something had fallen over. I went downstairs to find Fran in a full epileptic seizure, lying on the floor with a large amount of blood under her head. I called 911 and, even after the ambulance was gone, I was still shaking. Afterward, I was thinking about what, if any, effect this may have had on the baby.

Thankfully, the baby was okay!

In March of that year, my beautiful granddaughter was born, making it one of the greatest days of my life. Unbelievably, a wonderful thing came out of a terrible situation. The joy my granddaughter has brought to our lives is beyond description.

Eleanor married a great guy named Mick, and they have been very happy together for several years now. We have drawn closer through the years, though we can sometimes still push each other's buttons. She has a good head on her shoulders and has a keen sense of how to analyze people's problems and help them find solutions. I never had major concerns regarding her finding her way in life, and she has done well. I am very proud of her and thankful we have such a good relationship that has blossomed as she has progressed into adulthood.

From time to time, I would think about my mother, of the difficulties and pain she caused that led to the severing of our relationship. Despite all those terrible things she did to my siblings and me, I was finding sympathy for her somewhere in my heart. What drove that was how I had developed a deeper understanding of what caused her to suffer with the personality disorders she had.

Though I would still have moments of anger when remembering the things from the past that hurt, I also would feel sorry for her. I thought about how she should see her first and, at the time, only great grandchild. How that would be the right thing to do.

My sister called me, and we reconnected after several years apart. She was the go-between and first set up a call with my mother and daughters to talk over the phone. My daughters told my mother that they would only have a relationship if she spoke to me first and acknowledged what she had done.

When we spoke on the phone, I told her how I felt about the abuse, the pain that it caused me throughout my life, and how it made things exceedingly difficult for me. She apologized and I accepted.

That opened the door for her to meet her great-granddaughter, whom she loved until a few years later when she passed away. Though I'll never forget the terrible things she did to my siblings and me, I was glad that I was able to forgive her.

For some reason, I had always tried to correct things from my past at the later stages of my life. It was like some type of unfinished business, a retroactive fixing of things that had bothered me, and reconnecting with family was one of those things I felt I needed to correct. I think that perhaps just missing a reconnection with my uncle before he died was a big driver. How very wrong it was for all those relationships to be cut off by my parents!

I had not seen nor spoken to my father's side of the family since I was around fourteen years old. We were close in the early years before they found themselves in the web of my parent's hatred and resentment.

One day, I noticed that one of my first cousins had checked my LinkedIn profile. He was the youngest of the three children of my father's sister. I thought that it was interesting he did that and decided to try and contact him.

We ended up having a *great* conversation. Before we were about to hang up, he said his mother would like to talk to me. He then asked if that would be all right. I said, "Yes, absolutely!"

I remembered my aunt Sophie fondly. She and my uncle Simon (a famous comic-strip artist) had been a part of my life at a young age. I remembered my cousin Janis, one year older than me, playing a record for me the first time when I was five years old. I was amazed upon hearing Del Shannon's "Runaway" and thankful to Janis, who is an incredibly talented pianist and singer.

After a conversation with my aunt, Ann and I were invited to their house. Seeing them again after being cut off for so many years was simply wonderful. It was very emotional for me to hear their explanation of how bewildered they were that my parents had cut off the relationship. My dad was Aunt Sophie's only sibling, and she felt that a part of her family had been missing for years. She was so happy that reuniting with me and my siblings had, to some degree, helped fill that void.

We have had several get-togethers in the few years that followed, and what we all really enjoyed were the Thanksgiving mornings when I would go to their house. My cousins and their spouses were all there, and those were great times. I also reconnected with their older sister, my cousin Louise, and they were all so welcoming and loving toward me. We had some very good and deep conversations in which they expressed how painful it was for them when, suddenly, and after being so close, we were all gone from their lives.

I told them that I never really knew my grandparents on that side of the family, which was strange. My aunt told me that it was mainly due to my mother never allowing us to spend time with them. That was typical behavior for my mother, and we all lost out.

I greatly appreciated the reconnection which, to some degree, made up for the lost years. When my aunt would tell me how much she regretted all the things we missed out on, I would tell her that at least we had these last few years together.

She passed away a few years ago, and Uncle Simon moved up to Massachusetts. We still stay in touch and have seen each other a few times since. We always agree on how much we miss those Thanksgiving mornings spent together and how thankful we are for the reconnection.

CHAPTER 21

California Dream or Nightmare?

I was always interested in my family's history, but when I would ask my parents and grandparents where we came from, they would say Poland, Russia, Germany, or Lithuania, and provide little, if any, additional information. One line of the family on my mother's side had darker features, as did I, and we could pass for Italian, Spanish, or Middle Eastern.

I was intrigued by this and was able to find out some information about my great-grandmother via a relative I contacted by mail. This was prior to the internet. She had lived in a small town in Poland called Bilgoraj, and her father (my great-great grandfather) was from a line of seven generations who were all tailors. My mother filled in some blanks from stories she was told by the older relatives in her younger days. I started reading books and articles about the Jews in Eastern Europe to learn more, and when all the DNA testing started, I thought maybe that could help shed some more light on the mystery of my family's origins.

I anxiously awaited the results of my DNA test, and it finally arrived, revealing an interesting mix. The majority showed a broad category of "European Jew," which made sense. Jews remained highly insular during their exile, which was out of necessity in order to survive persecution and keep their religion and communities alive. The other percentages showed Iberian and Caucasus, and my mother's test (which I convinced her to take) also showed North African. A recent adjustment showed Central Asia and Mongolian for me and one other cousin on my mother's side. Though not precise, it seemed to explain a few things.

In addition to the DNA tests, I kept searching for more information and even visited gravesites of ancestors buried in the New York area to see what else I could find. I noticed that my great grandfather on my mother's side was a Kohen, which is from the priestly line. His wife, my great-grandmother, was the daughter of a Levite; the Levites were a separate group of workers in the ancient temples. I learned that through more recent DNA research, Kohens had a different genetic marker than other Jews. The line was passed down on the father's side, and thus it was determined that it goes back 160 generations.

One time, when a few family members were going through old family pictures, I saw one of a young man who looked very Italian or Spanish. I asked my mother who that was, and she said it was my great-grandfather. I was shocked, as I only remembered seeing him in other pictures when he was quite old. I later learned that through other DNA studies, it is believed that Jewish men had married Italian women. Jews were in Rome, some settling there as early as the fourth century, and others were taken there as slaves after Jerusalem was conquered (back around the time of Jesus).

Though much related to DNA research is debatable, this information may be the missing link and provide some answers to the questions I had.

I tracked other relatives through the ancestry testing service I used and was able to specifically identify family roots from Poland, Russia, and Lithuania. Several family names were German in origin, indicating that they lived there for a period of time. That is consistent with what many have concluded was one path the Jews had taken. That migration was from Rome to Germany and then east to the countries I was able to identify.

A really sad thing I learned was that my great-grandmother from another line of the family lost her whole family in the Holocaust. It was and remains like a huge puzzle, though what I learned makes a lot more sense than the short answers and lack of information I had previously received.

Another interesting thing the service provides are DNA matches whereby they match your DNA to other partici-pants to help identify potential family members. A messag-ing component allows members to communicate with each other to help discover what lost family may be out there. Many people have learned that this can be a mixed blessing, as some skeletons are potentially better left in closets, and my experience was no exception.

I received a message from a girl in which she mentioned noticing that she was a first-cousin DNA match to my mother and a second-cousin match to me. She said that she was adopted and had no idea who her biological parents were and asked if I could help. I was intrigued by this and went on a mission, as I was determined to help her and see what I could find out.

The only information from the girl, whose name was Regina, was that she was born in 1958 in Queens, New York, and was adopted by a family who lived in California. After talking to her on the phone, I found a site on which she had registered that was for people like her who were trying to locate their biological parents. In the brief description there, it mentioned that the father was an actor in Southern California who had abandoned the mother. That's all I had to go on.

I started by checking the family tree I had set up to try and identify people of the appropriate age to match up as potential parents. I then called my mother. She was also intrigued, though, at that time, she was losing her short-term memory. And yet she somehow could remember things from fifty years ago!

I had it narrowed down to three possibilities: two women and one man. Regarding the two women, my mother said, "They are possible; they were both tramps."

I laughed and asked her who this guy Sam was. She told me that he was a very good-looking guy and that all the cousins had crushes on him when they were young. She said he was a drummer who was an exceptionally good musician and that he and his family had moved to California several years ago.

Everything seemed to point to him as the father. I spoke again to Regina, and I told her about some of my family's physical features (i.e., dark, Middle Eastern, etc.). She told me that it was the same with her. I needed to find out more information and see if we could fully confirm our theory.

I noticed from the family tree that Sam had a niece and nephew who I remembered meeting in Brooklyn when I was around seven years old. They were both in town for the wedding of one of my uncles.

I tried to contact the guy who I believed was my cousin living in California. I sent him an email and left a voice mail, explaining a little bit about why I was contacting him. He did not respond. I kept at it, and, after searching intensely for a few weeks, I found who I thought was my cousin, Sam's niece, living in Vegas. I called the number, figuring I had nothing to lose.

A guy answered, and when I explained who I was, he said, "Let me put Marnie on the phone."

She was shocked to hear from me and remembered us playing together in my grandmother's basement when we were kids. I explained a little about why I was contacting her and I asked, "Is it possible that Sam is this girl's father?"

"It's one-thousand percent possible," she said. "Let me put my husband Greg on the phone."

Greg and I spoke for around two hours, during which time he told me all about Sam, story after story. The guy I thought was just some old guy on the family tree was someone entirely different. He was a terribly angry tough guy and ladies' man who had some unsavory connections (to say the least). There were stories about his adventures with women, fights, gun toting, anger, and more.

My mother had told me that Sam had a fight with Jerry Lewis, which I attributed to the dementia and ignored. Still, I asked Greg if Sam ever had a fight with Jerry Lewis.

"He kicked the shit out of Jerry Lewis," he replied.

Sam was Lewis's bodyguard at the time, and the story was that they got into a dispute over some nonsense, which led to the beatdown.

Another incident occurred when one of their friends, an elderly gentlemen, was kidnapped by some thugs who were demanding a ransom. They told Sam about it, and all he asked for was the address. He returned not only with the guy who was being held but also with a sum of money greater than the amount of the ransom.

There were also a few interesting things that revealed Sam's more positive side. Sam did some drumming for Frank Sinatra, who had different drummers come in and out of the bands who backed him up. Another was that he was a friend of Sam Cooke, the famous singer who was murdered at a young age.

After the lengthy conversation, my head was spinning. Not only were the missing pieces regarding Regina's biological father pretty much confirmed, but it also revealed to me a whole other side of my family that in some weird way made sense.

I asked Greg if Sam knew or ever hung out with my uncle Hal the dentist, and he told me that he did and that Hal would go out to California and hang out with him for periods of time. They were so different in their personalities that it is hard to comprehend a friendship between them. That raised some questions that will never be answered now that they are both gone.

Sam, though not a major player, was one of the "Tough Jews" referenced in the title of a book that was written about Jewish mobsters. That list included Meyer Lansky, Bugsy Siegal, Lefty Rosenthal, and many others who were mean, violent guys.

I had always thought that I was the exception to the family regarding my behavior in my teen years, yet here was this guy who made me seem like a choir boy. It was quite interesting to learn about him, and I regret that I never got to meet or know him. It somehow made a lot of sense that a guy like that was a close blood relative.

Greg told me that Sam had passed away at the age of sixty-seven after being diagnosed with cancer. He had refused medical attention and never went to a doctor.

I heard several more stories before I was able to meet Regina while on a business trip to LA. She was very appreciative of my help in identifying one of her biological parents. It eventually led her to meeting her half sister, which was confirmed by DNA. She also met her half brother, Sam's ex-wife, and a few cousins. The whole thing brought some closure and happiness to her, though when all was said and done, she told me, "I am so glad that I was raised by my adoptive parents."

CHAPTER 22

Who Says You Can't Go Home?

At times throughout the years, I would envision what work would be like toward the latter part of my career. I pictured a corner office in New York City with a pleasant view and how that would be a time in which I could sit back and manage things in a more relaxed manner.

It didn't turn out that way.

The last eight years wound up in many ways as the most productive and stressful of my entire career. Amid the never-ending meetings, long hours, and intense travel, I achieved many of the goals I had set for myself early on, but it came at a cost.

People say you know when it's time to retire, and I found that to be true. The decision was not an easy one, as I knew I would be leaving an exceptionally good job with many positives. I had worked so hard to get to a certain level, and it made me wonder how I could walk away. However, toward the very end, I knew deep down that I did not want to do it anymore. Though I would be jumping into the unknown, I was always one to take chances.

My colleagues gave me a wonderful farewell, and it was great to hear the stories they each told regarding the various interactions we had shared. It was like I was being roasted, and some of those stories were quite amusing.

The team that I managed had a separate meeting in which each person took a turn to speak about our time working together. I was deeply touched to hear the positive impact I had made on each of them. Helping others is something very special and meaningful to me, so it was very gratifying to hear how I was able to achieve that. I will never forget them or the tribute they gave me.

Retirement began with my mother getting extremely sick. She suffered from dementia and other illnesses. She wound up in a hospital and was approaching the end when COVID-19 was in full swing, so we could not visit her in person. The nurses were kind enough to set up two Zoom calls, and though she was barely coherent during the calls, when I told her I loved her, she uttered, "I hope so."

When I spoke at the graveside during the funeral, I focused only on the positive things I remembered about her. It was a good list, and, as I spoke, I remembered those things from when I was a little boy, and I broke down in tears. I felt sorry for her that her emotional problems prevented her from living a fuller and happier life.

All the family members I reconnected with had loved her despite how she had destroyed all the relationships. The tragedy of everything that happened was how much my parents were loved, yet they were never capable of appreciating that. The damage they did to their children and the pain they inflicted upon us was severe and had long-lasting effects. Those effects never fully go away and are difficult (if not impossible) to totally forget, though they can be managed.

My mother's death was obviously not a great start to retirement, but several good things were right around the corner.

During the pandemic, a few of my musician friends who were stuck at home during the lockdown were posting short videos of themselves playing some guitar riffs. One day I decided to do one, and I thought it was okay. I decided to post it and see if anybody would even watch it. I had my doubts, but I figured what the hell?

After I posted it, the responses were overwhelmingly positive. My friend Cappy, whom I had last played with nine years prior, commented, "When this shit is over, we have to jam."

People say that quite often, though it rarely (if ever) happens. Newly retired, I contacted him to just have lunch and explore maybe having a jam session.

It was a typical early February day in Queens when I headed down Lakeville Road and turned right on Union Turnpike. The memories started flooding back as I made my way to the block where I grew up.

When I stopped in front of my old house, the feeling was one of sadness, and thoughts of my mother who had recently passed came to mind. I stared at the house in which so many of my growing-up years took place. It seemed so small. I saw a big air-conditioner like the one I had in my small upstairs bedroom, and it brought back many memories from the time I lived in that room so many years ago.

Going down the narrow streets and avoiding the piles of snow that created just one lane on the road made me wonder how we ever drove anywhere during the huge snowstorms of our youth.

Over to Little Neck Parkway and heading south, the houses looked pretty much as I remembered them. Maybe there was one "McMansion," the new wave of houses being built that stand out like sore thumbs among the Capes.

Going past the Garden Apartments on Tulip Avenue where Ann and her family lived when we were engaged and so young, I remembered how I would wait out front in my car to pick her up. Across the street was the library, which was the "internet" before there was one. It was where I used to go and spend time researching things of interest.

Seeing the Long Island Railroad station, the apartment Ann and I lived in briefly on the south side, and the house where I had the amazing year of guitar lessons with Larry all brought back parts of my life that were precious. It was surreal to be back there after the journey I had been on.

Cappy and I had a nice lunch and were walking to our cars when I asked about maybe getting together for a jam with some of the Turtle Guys. He said he also had something else, another situation. He explained that guys he had been playing with for years had lost their guitar player, who had moved away. He asked if I wanted to come down and jam and see how it went. Maybe it would be a one-time thing or an occasional jam. Whatever the case, I agreed, and we set a date.

As I was driving home with the New Riders song "Whiskey" playing, I was exhilarated. After years working and traveling around the world and all the incredible experiences I had, I was somehow home again.

The initial jam went pretty well, and they asked me if I wanted to do it again. We wound up playing together for a year and a half, and it's been a lot of fun. They are all very good musicians who have been playing together on and off for many years. The singer has an exceptionally good voice, and we all meshed well, which very often is a problem with bands and egos. I learned a tremendous amount from the experience, as they covered a wide range of classic rock songs. I had to learn many different styles, and, as a result, it significantly expanded my skill set.

The drummer made several videos of our practices and posted them on social media. The reactions and comments, mostly from friends and family, were very positive. Several people who commented asked when we would play at a venue. That was not really the main objective, though I was hoping that maybe at some point we would do that. We weren't getting any younger, and just moving all the equipment around was something we did not look forward to.

Unexpectedly, we were asked to play at a private engagement party, followed by a gig at the Fourth of July Stewart

Manor Street Fair. We agreed, and, at fairly short notice to prepare, we were able to put together enough material to play seven hours combined for around forty different songs.

It went quite well. There is nothing better than playing live. I am not sure if it will continue, but, when it ends, I will look back with very positive memories of the entire experience. Having hobbies is a key to a successful retirement, and playing with those guys has been a great experience.

Shortly before I retired, my second granddaughter was born, and what a joy she has been. She exhibits intelligence and a sense of humor and keeps us greatly entertained. My grandchildren and daughters have brought Ann and me incredible happiness. Eleanor and Mark had moved in with us after their cross-country trip was cut short due to COVID-19 having erupted soon after they ventured out. Having my family close to us has been another major factor in the enjoyment of my retirement.

I also find that I am still reconnecting with extended family. My aunt Barbara is the only sibling of my mother still alive. She reached out when my mother died, and we had an incredible conversation. She and my mother's brothers were connections that were especially important to me. I always treasured the memories with them from when I was a toddler in my grandmother's house during those critical formative years. Despite those relationships having been destroyed by my mother, I firmly believe that they were a major factor in helping me to survive and thrive throughout life's difficulties.

In the years leading up to and since retiring, I have lost several friends and, most recently, Uncle Herb, the other brother of my mother. Three work colleagues passed at fairly young ages, and I think, in those cases, work stress may have factored in. The list of Big I and Turtle Guys who passed has grown in the last few years, and, recently, two more have left us. It is the sad part of life, though a silver lining is the recognition and deeper appreciation of the time we have left.

Several reunion gatherings and memorials have drawn friends from the old neighborhood closer together at this later stage of life.

I did not know what to expect in the next chapter when I made the difficult decision to retire. The freedom to do what I want, when I want, and the release from the heavy work pressures is what I have been wanting for a long time. Marrying so young placed financial pressures on us from day one, and that was a long time ago. Time with family, reconnections, friends (both old and new), reading, music, golf, pool, grandkids—all have provided me with a long-desired level of contentment.

At the time of this writing, it is unfortunate that our country is divided, in turmoil, and that the world is suffering with wars, pain, and destruction. The suffering that people go through is devastating to see. It touches raw nerves for me and at times brings a sense of hopelessness, seeing innocent people being murdered or having their lives destroyed.

Though I find it difficult to achieve, and it seems to be a lifelong struggle, I try to find meaning in the suffering that people are enduring. It has been the history of man and asking why will not provide any real answer.

Suffering is a painful reality of the human condition. Viktor Frankl, a neurologist, psychiatrist, philosopher, author, and Holocaust survivor, was recommended to me by Dr. K when I was struggling to understand what the meaning of life was. I read a few of Frankl's books, and the main message I came away with are the following things regarding what provides meaning to a person's life: What one experiences, the work one does, and their attitude about suffering, inevitably comes to everyone, regardless of where one believes it comes from. Frankl described how he was able to derive meaning even from his time in a concentration camp by ministering to and helping others.[5] That same message can be found in several religious, philosophical, and psychological writings.

Several years ago, while attending a bat mitzvah for the daughter of my wife's friend, the rabbi gave an interesting sermon. He spoke about Jethro, the father-in-law of Moses.

Although there is much debate regarding details of Jethro's background, it is believed that prior to meeting Moses, he had experimented with all the other religions and beliefs of his time. He also had several names he was known by. That rabbi spoke about how, by interacting with many diverse cultures and their beliefs, Jethro became someone who truly knew God.

That left a great impression upon me because at that time, through my work, I had interacted with people from many distinct cultures and was starting to travel internationally.

Those travels became an integral part of my journey as they opened the door for me to experience many different cultures and interact with people from twenty-two countries around the world. I learned about their customs, religious beliefs, and approaches to life. The journey that started in my grandmother's house in Brooklyn, New York, took me through Asia, Europe, the Middle East, and Latin America. I stared out at the South China Sea from the former Subic Bay Naval Base in the Philippines. I rode a camel and toured the desert in Dubai. I saw the building in Munich, Germany, where Neville Chamberlain and Adolph Hitler signed the Munich Pact in 1938. I toured the House of Commons in London. I found the oldest synagogue in Europe while spending a magnificent week in Barcelona. Those were just some of the amazing and unforgettable experiences I was fortunate enough to have in my life.

Some religions teach reincarnation, that people are reborn and live many lifetimes until they learn all their souls need to. There have also been several cases of near-death experiences documented and written about by reputable physicians. Though nothing has been proven regarding these things, I strongly feel as if I have lived several different lifetimes within my present life, learning many invaluable lessons along the way.

I survived the pain, confusion, and trauma caused by the abuse I was subjected to throughout my childhood and teen years. The help I received through friends and, in some cases, their families, was a major factor in helping me get through it all. The nine years I spent in a cult somehow created many positives, as I learned things about my religion and other religions that I never would have otherwise. It also helped me develop business and management skills that were immensely valuable in my career.

Through it all, I either possessed or developed the trait of grit—courage, strength of character, and the determination to lift oneself up after getting knocked down. According to many experts and studies, grit is the main characteristic that determines success in life.

My wife had to put up with all the emotional damage I suffered, and she stayed by my side through it all. Though we have had our ups and downs over the years, our marriage has endured, and she has been my rock, the one person who has loved me unconditionally, the one whom I could always depend on to be there for me. Together, we were able to build our family—two wonderful daughters and my two granddaughters—whom I love beyond what words could ever say.

I always knew that, deep down, I was a good and decent person. Yet knowing that while hearing all the terrible things my parents would say about me created an inner conflict. Not knowing how to deal with that is what caused the anger to develop. I believe that subconsciously I wanted and needed to prove to myself and others . . . that

I was not that terrible person my mother had created in her own mind. That the bad things I did and went through in my youth were not who I really was. It created a driving force within me to succeed in all aspects of life, primarily by being a good person to all of my friends, neighbors, colleagues, and family members. Secondarily, it drove me to succeed in my career, recreational activities, and hobbies, such as music and sports. I had a huge battle to fight in order to correct things from the past, and, though the work is ongoing, I believe I have thus far succeeded.

Every person has their own path in life, and mine took me from the lowest of lows to great heights. I did not choose the things that happened to me or the experiences I had along the way. Through it all, there was something inside that kept driving me forward. I am thankful for the life I have had up until now, and, though I do not know what lies ahead, I know I'm up to the task. The unknown is what makes life interesting.

I remain optimistic about the time I have left to travel on the path down the highway, and I have evolved into what one of our great leaders once said, "I'm an idealist without illusions."[6]

> *There is a road, no simple highway*
> *Between the dawn and dark of night*
> *And if you go, no one may follow*
> *That path is for your steps alone . . .*

—Robert Hunter/Jerry Garcia[7]

ACKNOWLEDGMENTS

*T*his book is the story I wanted to tell to help expose the child abuse and trauma that can exist behind closed doors. If understanding what I endured and how I was able to recover helps even one person, then I believe it was well worth the effort.

I would like to extend a special thanks to Amanda Morris, who generously gave her time to provide a first round of editing. Your positive and honest feedback gave me the confidence to continue.

I would also like to thank Robert Miranda, an old friend, for leading me to a fantastic publishing services team of Melinda Martin and Gail Fallen, who were both a pleasure to work with.

To Dr. David Kirschner, who helped me in so many ways and is the main catalyst in helping me to recover: You planted the seed that my story had value, which led to my writing this book.

Thanks, too, to my dear friends Bill Morris and Jerry Duci, who provided encouragement every step of the way . . . and to *all* the friends from my youth who were always there for me when I needed it most.

To Rena Lipiner Katz, I will always remain grateful for your encouragement and inspiration.

And to my wife, children, and granddaughters: You fill my heart with more joy and happiness than words could ever express.

Rory D. Kaplan

Rory D. Kaplan was born in Brooklyn and grew up in Queens, New York. He started working various part-time jobs at age fifteen that taught him discipline and self-sufficiency. He put himself through college while working and married with two children. He had a long and successful career in which he held a variety of positions in both information technology and trade finance banking.

His work led him to travel extensively within the US and twenty-two countries around the world. As a result, he was able to interact with people from many different backgrounds and cultures, something which broadened his perspective and enriched his life experience.

He lives with his wife in New York and is currently enjoying retired life with his family, friends, music, and writing.

NOTES

1   See Leonard Shengold, *Soul Murder: The Effects of Childhood Abuse and Deprivation* (New York: Random House, 1991).

2   Kimberlee Roth and Freda B. Friedman, *Surviving a Borderline Parent: How to Heal Your Childhood Wounds & Build Trust, Boundaries, and Self-Esteem* (Oakland, CA: New Harbinger, 2004) 3.

3   Allan Schwartz, "The Borderline Personality Disordered Family: Part II: The Children," Allan Schwartz's Weblog, *MentalHealth.net,* April 4, 2007, https://www.mentalhelp .net/blogs/the-borderline-personality-disordered-family-part -ii-the-children/.

4   John Hubner and Lindsey Gruson, *Monkey on a Stick: Murder, Madness, and the Hare Krishnas* (Boston: Harcourt, 1988), 392.

5   Viktor Frankl, *Man's Search for Meaning* (Boston: Beacon Press, 2006), Kindle.

6   John F. Kennedy, quoted in Arthur Schlessinger, *A Thousand Days: John F. Kennedy in the White House* (Boston: Mariner Books, 2002), 7.

7   The Grateful Dead, "Ripple," Robert Hunter (lyrics) and Jerry Garcia (music), track six, on *American Beauty* (Los Angeles: Warner Bros.), 1970.